WORSHIPPER WARRIOR

A 21-DAY JOURNEY INTO THE DANGEROUS LIFE OF DAVID

STEVE HOLT

Worshipper Warrior Press
2025 Parliament Dr.
Colorado Springs 80920
info@theroad.org

Praise For Worshipper Warrior

Steve Holt's book on the life of David will transform lives! I know Steve personally, and I can say he speaks from real-life experience. Chapter 14 on Intimacy will help anyone who faces adversity.

Congressman Doug Lamborn, U.S. Representative for Colorado's 5th Congressional District

These 21 chapters are a personal and practical life map for a glorious journey toward radical transformation. Steve Holt invites us to dive deep into the character and story of David to discover how we, too, can become men after God's own heart: men who are fully alive in Christ and decidedly devoted to a passionate—even reckless—pursuit of the Lord. This is not a coffee table devotional for mere moments of quiet reflection; each of these 21-Days is a substantive step toward real and lasting life change. Do not approach *Worshipper Warrior* casually. Prepare your heart with a vision for the man you want to become, and then allow the Lord to mold you thoroughly in His likeness as each page and life lesson unfolds.

Dick Eastman, International President, Every Home for Christ, best-selling author

I recently had the privilege of guiding Steve on a Colorado Elk Hunt. Deep in the woods of the San Juan Mountains, I discovered Steve's heart for men and the strengthening of their walks with God…Steve lays out the story of David, and he shows us what it looks like to be a real man of God, to fight like a warrior and worship wholeheartedly. The "Blood Stained Allies" section of the book was so encouraging for me. I highly recommend this book; it has changed my life and it will change your life too.

Rick Webb, Big Game Hunter and Guide, Founder Dark Timber Outfitters

It is amazing to me that a present-day pastor could identify David as the greatest king in the world. David's struggles with temptation and the Holy Spirit's work in his life were overwhelming. However, that is exactly what Steve Holt has done in his new book. I highly recommend this book for both its content and encouragement. Enjoy!

Dwight Johnson, Author, *Transparent Leadership*, Founder, Men with a Purpose

The journey that you take as you flip through the pages of this book is nothing short of eye opening. Pastor Steve Holt really dives deep into the life of David to a whole new level

I've never seen before, the true wholehearted life that David lived and through the real-life experiences Pastor Steve went through really shows us how deep God's love for us is. Even though David lived an imperfect life, Pastor Steve dives into the true meaning of a worshiper and warrior and how David's life perfectly portrays that. This book is a must read for all godly men who want to truly walk out a wholehearted life for Christ.

Justin Stuart, YouTube Influencer, MoreJStu, over three million subscribers

I had the privilege of being a part of Steve's discipleship group with a few other young men. Steve's heart for men was so evident, and this book is just what the men in this generation need as fuel to become warriors for God. I would highly recommend this book to anyone who is NOT a perfect person (all of us.) Through all of David's accolades and faults, his heart for God was the most important thing, and we can all follow that.

Andrew Scites, YouTube Influencer, MoreJStu, over three million subscribers

This book is a must for any man…I strongly suggest taking this 21-day challenge. When you do, I'm confident it will be a life changer—it was for me! I have been a Christian for over 35 years, have read and listened to countless sermons and books on what it takes to be a "Godly man," but *Worshipper Warrior* not only breaks the mold by clearly and accurately describing King David's victories and failures, it correspondingly presents real-world examples of real-life experiences that speak directly to what a true warrior for Christ looks like.

Jeffrey A Paulk, US Air Force fighter pilot, Colonel (retired)

This book is so real, so well-written, so biblical, and so practical. Steve's knowledge of God's Word and history, coupled with his transparency and down-to-earth practicality makes this a must read for all men. Not to mention, Steve is just an excellent writer. Oh, women might want to read it also, just because it is so good. You will never be the same after these 21-Days!

Dr. David Holt, Author, *Pastoring with Passion*, Founder and Sr. Pastor of Living Hope Church, Athens, GA.

I have known Pastor Steve for over 15 years and he is a man of prayer. Praying people are warriors and Steve is a warrior…There are not many books calling for Christian men to be courageous prayer warriors. This book does just that. For every man who desires to make a difference, to lead their families well and to live as a faithful witness, the 21-day challenge is for them. I strongly recommend this timely book and would encourage Churches to use this tool to help their men grow into courageous warriors for Christ.

Arjuna Chiguluri, Founder & CEO of Vision Nationals India, Nepal, and Thailand.

Worshipper Warrior is a gut-level exploration of God's heart to meet men in the midst of their deepest needs. Pastor Steve leads us on a journey through the life of David, the consummate man's man…Steve deals with issues like suffering, vulnerability, betrayal, passion, and many others are addressed with the goal of bringing us into a deeper trust in the God who loves us, and a greater commitment to moving forward in confidence that He is leading us ever onward, and ever upward!

Pastor Brian Michaels, Pastor, Springs Lighthouse, Colorado Springs, CO

Reading Steve's book, I discovered deep insights into a man's warrior heart through intensely deep dives into Scripture. That synchronized my heart to Biblical Principles of masculinity. Often asking 'where's the beef' in most books for men, the beef of God's Word permeates this manly, wise, insightful view of Worshippers and Warriors.

Jay Inman, US Army, Lieutenant Colonel, Retired, Author of nine fiction books including *Walking at the Top of the World*

In a world where men are emasculated, my heart sang as I read through Pastor Steve's book which not only captures the warrior heart of men but the tender, compassionate side as well. His book gives me a greater understanding of the struggles men face and the compass to bring them back to wholehearted living! We walked the road with Pastor Steve that inspired this book, born out of great adversity. This journey is real, raw and redeemed. Women can gain a deeper understanding of the men in their lives through reading this book and yes even gain great insight for themselves.

Jan Inman, Wife, Home School mom, Author and Illustrator of children's book, *Little Lamb*

"I have seen first-hand the tremendous impact that this book has had in the lives of men, both men who knew they were broken and men who had yet to discover that fact. This book brings the masculine heart to a place of rescue and restoration. It gives permission to face the shame in our lives and take the challenge to be a wholehearted Worshipper, Warrior, and Disciple of Jesus Christ. It's changing men's lives!"

Ryan Styre, Pastor @ The Road, Co-Founder and Senior Cadre of Worshipper & Warrior Ministries

Dedication

To the men who gathered around my fire pit at Hebron Woods in my darkest hour.

To my deepest counselors, Liz, and our passionate family.

To the Cadre, who first heard and critiqued the concepts of this book.

To the members of The Road who have been willing
to follow a leader who walks with a limp.

To Kent Miller who continually provides wise counsel
in my journey toward wholehearted living.

To the creative strategy team that made this book a reality: Ryan Styre, Jay Inman, Karla Dial, Anna Holt, Pam Doyon, Jan Inman, Michael Brymer, and Isaac Holt.

"As for the saints who are on the earth,
They are the excellent ones,
In whom is all my delight"

A Michtam of David

Psalm 16:3

Table of Contents

Dedication vi

FOREWORD viii

A GUIDE TO READING THIS BOOK: THE 21-DAY CHALLENGE 9

INTRODUCTION 11

DAY 1: WHOLEHEARTED 16

DAY 2: INTERVIEW 23

DAY 3: OIL 33

DAY 4: WORSHIPPER 42

DAY 5: CAUSE 52

DAY 6: WARRIOR 64

DAY 7: LIONS 74

DAY 8: ENEMIES 83

DAY 9: ALLIES 93

DAY 10: WILDERNESS 103

DAY 11: INQUIRY 111

DAY 12: COURAGE 119

DAY 13: REFUGE 127

DAY 14: INTIMACY 135

DAY 15: CONDITIONS 143

DAY 16: IDENTITY 152

DAY 17: PASSION 162

DAY 18: COMPROMISE 171

DAY 19: SUFFERING 181

DAY 20: POET 192

DAY 21: LEGACY 200

ENDNOTES 210

FOREWORD

Not another Men's book! I will be uncomfortably truthful: I'm not a fan of most devotionals for men. Why? Most were not written to create a ruggedness of soul and challenge men to be warriors, but rather just make us "good."

If you are like me and don't want to be known or remembered as a "good man" but rather, "good at being a Man," then this is a book for you and all men's groups! It's the hard-hitting truth, tempered with constant encouragement in this book that helped me face ISIS on a number of missions recovering and helping orphans and living the Gospel in Iraq. But let's face it, most men are not going to Iraq to risk dying as Christians or seeking to obey the Lord in austere environments. In some ways, I think it's harder just living your faith in good old America. That's why I highly recommend this book and commend my longtime friend and blood-stained ally Steve Holt!

Victor Marx
High Risk Missionary
President
All Things Possible Ministries

A GUIDE TO READING THIS BOOK: THE 21-DAY CHALLENGE

Would it surprise you if I told you that watching hours of reality TV will not dramatically raise your IQ? Or that a New Year's Resolution usually doesn't translate into weight loss? Probably not. But we all know we should exercise, sleep eight hours a night, eat healthier, and even read our Bibles. But does this knowledge make doing them any easier?

Of course not. Because in life, knowledge is only part of the battle. Without action, knowledge is meaningless. This book is about actually changing your actions, not just knowing that you should.

But if you have a passion to be a worshipper and warrior; if you have a desire to become a man who is dangerous; if you have a hunger to be a man after God's own heart—like David—it will take twenty-one days to activate the energy needed to form the new man inside you.

Maxwell Maltz was a plastic surgeon who began noticing a strange pattern among his patients in the 1950s. When Maltz performed an operation—like a nose job, for example—he found it took the patient about twenty-one days to get used to seeing his or her new face. Similarly, when a patient had an arm or a leg amputated, Maltz noticed the patient would sense a phantom limb for about twenty-one days before adjusting to the new situation.

These experiences prompted Maltz to think about his own adjustment period to changes and new behaviors, and noticed he also took about twenty-one days to form a new habit. "These, and many other commonly observed phenomena," Maltz later wrote, "tend to show that it requires a minimum of about twenty-one days for an old mental image to dissolve and a new one to jell."[1]

Similarly, Shawn Achor, in his best-selling book *The Happiness Advantage* (Crown Business Books, 2010), speaks of "activation energy" as the key to forming a new habit. He explains it this way:

> In physics, activation energy is the initial spark needed to catalyze a reaction. The same energy, both physical and mental, is needed of people to overcome inertia and kick start a positive habit.[2]

Achor had always wanted to learn to play the guitar. He found it took twenty seconds to walk over to his closet, pull the guitar out and begin to practice. Those twenty seconds, combined with twenty-one days of practice, was the ticket to a new habit and a new joy.

Thus, the twenty-one-day challenge for men. This book has been set up to be read in twenty-one days—one chapter per day. Each chapter starts with a Bible passage to read before beginning the chapter and ends with a few questions. Knowing that men are busy with jobs, family, and leisure activities, I've designed each reading, with questions, to take about thirty minutes. Thirty minutes for twenty-one days is a small investment to change your life.

I hope you'll take the challenge and discover a new way of thinking and a new outlook on life. If you can invest thirty minutes for just twenty-one days, it won't be long before you're reaping the benefits. The first step is to find a quiet place to read and enjoy the dangerous adventure of the life of David!

INTRODUCTION

The Bible never flatters its heroes.[3] The Bible is primarily a story of men—but not the kind of men we hear about in our churches today. These are not the men whose most important job in the church is handing out bulletins on Sunday morning. The Bible is raw and honest about its heroes. And among them all, David stands out.

There is more about David's personal life than anyone in the Bible; he is the most real, passionate, bawdy man in all of Scripture. Other than Jesus, there is no one about whose heart intentions and motivations we're told more than David's. This is no polished view of a man, but a ragged-edged reality in which we see humanness and manliness being formed with much coarseness—a spiritual and earthy man who is full of emotion and honesty.

Indeed, the songs of David, the Psalms that best reflect his heart longings and motivations, are on the one hand sublimely beautiful, rapturous poems about God and on the other, almost vicious cries for vengeance against his enemies. Guttural, honest heart cries. By our modern standards of psychological evaluation, David might be diagnosed as bipolar!

God Hunger

But let's be thoroughly honest: David is much like us. If we can cut through the religious posturing and overly spiritualized vernacular of our modern church mindset, we might see ourselves for who we are—lustful, driven, depressed, anxious, and longing for something to live for. What makes David different? He's after God. He is seeking God's passions, God's emotions, God's purposes. He's relentless. David is anything but passive.

The Scriptures tell us David is a man after God's own heart (1 Samuel 13:14; Acts 13:22). It's fascinating that as we delve into his life, we discover not a perfect man with altar-boy motivations, but rather a robust, passionate longing for God that unnerves us and even challenges our starchy, clear-cut boundaries of religious protocol. This is a man after God's own heart? This is a man who will do all of God's will? God's heart in a man looks much different than what we've come to believe.

This is a man with a heart set free! Not a man of perfection and predictable responses; no, David is a man of deep devotion and deep faults. David is a man who has a passionate heart and bloodied hands. He is a worshipper and a warrior. But, at the end of the day, he has, more than anything else, a hunger for God. Eugene Peterson says it this way:

> God is who we need; the God-hunger, the God-thirst is the most powerful drive in us. It's far stronger than all the drives of sex, power, security, and fame put together. And the David story is the most complete, detailed rendering of God-dimensioned humanity that we have, the common life that God uses to shape humanity to His glory.[4]

This book is for men, and David is the most relatable man in the Bible. Like each of us, he is a saint and sinner. David is a man after God's holy heart who is seeking Him with a sinful heart. Martin Luther described Christians as "simultaneously saint and sinner"—and redefines "saint" to mean "forgiven sinner." We are called saints, not because we change into something different, but because our relationship with God changes through God's grace. Luther said: "The saints are sinners, too, but they are forgiven and absolved."

Saint and Sinner

No one in the whole Bible so completely lived a life as saint and sinner as David. David deals with God and lets God deal with him! He is a surrendered sinner! David is crushed under sin and overwhelmed by God's grace. He is passionate in his love for God and passionate in his love for women; can any of us modern men relate?

David is a fantastically courageous warrior on the battlefield, but a coward in parenting his children. David is pure and sacrificial in his motives with his motley band of men but is lustful and conniving in his pursuit of a married woman. Yet, ironically, David is full of God and God is all for David.

When God is directing Samuel to look at another man to lead Israel in place of Saul, he describes the young shepherd this way: "The LORD has sought for Himself a man after His own heart, and the LORD has commanded him *to be* commander over His people."[5] God's view of David was that of a worshipper and warrior, both a tender poet and a freedom fighter, simultaneously a seeker after God's heart and a contending champion over his people.

True Manliness

Could it be that David is a witness to us of the kind of heart, the kind of person, even the kind of leader, that God desires? Why so much about David in the Bible? Why so many glimpses into his personal life?

Why not?

God has a message for us today, a witness of a type of man that is passionate yet flawed, purposeful yet misguided, worshipful yet angry, a warrior yet a coward. Isaiah speaks of his witness to all of us.

> *Incline your ear, and come to Me.*
> *Hear, and your soul shall live;*
> *And I will make an everlasting covenant with you—*
> *The sure mercies of David.*
> *Indeed I have given him as a witness to the people,*
> *A leader and commander for the people.*
> **Isaiah 55: 3-4**

David is anything but religious. He makes us uncomfortable; his heart cries are so dang human, so passionate, so manly. Yet the prophet Isaiah says he is a "witness to the people." I believe, maybe against conventional religious wisdom, that David is a prophetic witness of godly manliness. Could it be that David is a type of Jesus-follower, a type of leader, a type of wholehearted man that is needed today?

David is a witness to the men of the twenty-first century. We need Davidic men with Davidic hearts in our time.

Do you realize there are more disciples of Christ alive today than all of history combined? That means there are more Jesus-followers on the earth right now than are currently in Heaven. Might we be in the latter days, the final count, before the coming of the Lord? Is a harvest of unprecedented proportions coming soon? Is God about to populate Heaven like never in history? Is God raising up a new kind of disciple, a new breed of leader, a new type of man, that will see David as a kind of witness to the Last Days Church?

God doesn't look at people the way man does; He doesn't consider the outward appearance, but gazes at the heart (1 Samuel 16:7). There is a need today for a new anointing, a new covering of grace, over the heart of the people of God. For it is from the heart that we live, parent, lead, love, care, forgive. We desperately need the sure mercies of David's heart over our lives, our leadership, and our churches.

A Dangerous Man

David was a dangerous man! This book you have in your hand is designed to make you a dangerous man, too. I have chosen twenty-one aspects of David's life, in chronological order—from his humble beginnings as the youngest in his family, shepherding his father's livestock to his death as a king—all relating to being human, to being a man, to being a truly dangerous man of God. Each chapter points the reader to the greatest man who ever lived—Jesus.

I have assigned questions to be answered at the end of each chapter. I believe this book could change your life. I say that because it was in my most desperate days, my most broken moments, that God mightily used David in my life. As I read the story of David again and again, I rediscovered my masculine heart. If you are hungry for more, if you are longing for God, the same can happen to you.

God is the same yesterday, today, and tomorrow, and He is still looking for and connecting His heart to men who will seek Him wholeheartedly. Moses wrote, "You will seek the LORD your God, and you will find *Him* if you seek Him with all your heart and with all your soul."[6] David is an example to us of a heart on fire, a heart set free.

If you are God-starved, God-hungry, God-thirsty—or just wondering if your heart can take another crushing defeat, another failed relationship—then David is your man. David, a man very much like us and yet so very different from us, can take us into a new heart discovery of wild freedom.

Dr. Steve Holt, DD, MA

Colorado Springs, Colorado

DAY 1: WHOLEHEARTED

1 Samuel 13
*14 The Lord has sought for Himself a man after His own heart, and the
Lord has commanded him to be commander over His people.*

I didn't learn to read until I was eleven years old. I could mouth the words on the page before that, but I didn't learn to read—*really* read—until I was in fifth grade. I had a teacher, Mrs. Milton, who might have been the first to notice some potential within my mouthy, brash life. Before that, the teachers at my elementary school knew me more by the back of my head than the front of my face. Always in trouble for talking too much and listening too little, I was passed from grade to grade to give the previous teacher a break. But Mrs. Milton taught me to love reading.

When that happened, I fell in love with biographies. Real-life stories enraptured me. Fiction was fable and myth, too squishy, too illusory—but biography? Now, that was the stuff of actual courage. These were the stories of common men of uncommon exploits. I lived vicariously through the adventures of Davy Crockett, Daniel Boone, and Hugh Glass. I couldn't get enough of Lewis and Clark, the Corps of Discovery Expedition, Teddy Roosevelt, or a Bible guy named David.

At bedtime, my mom would read Bible stories to me. I can still see the picture book she used. I heard stories about Abraham, Moses, and the other characters in Scripture. But David took pride of place in my memory. I can still see the picture of him on the page—beardless, youthful, muscular, wearing nothing but a loincloth, loosely holding a sling with a poised confidence and athletic demeanor that looked like a cocky pitcher standing on the mound about to throw the third strike. He didn't seem like a Bible character at all. He seemed too human, too rugged, too young. He captured my heart. From that day on, David was the one figure in the Bible I could relate to.

Fully Alive

Nothing against Abraham, Samuel, or Elijah, but they just seemed old, even ancient, due to the gray beards and wrinkled, weathered faces in the picture book. But David? He was different. The stories about him seemed to be full of blood, bravery, and intrigue. Drama. David stories were daring, rebellious, and well, kind of what I wanted to be... wild, dangerous, and full of passion. I wanted to be like him!

What I didn't know at the time, but learned later, was that the Bible has more information about David's personality, character, and life than anyone else's. His is the most extensively narrated story in all of Scripture. That's no accident. Arguably, apart from Jesus, no other person in the Bible exhibits such wholehearted, passionate devotion to God as David. Irenaeus, the first-century church father, might have been talking about David when he wrote, "the glory of God is a man fully alive." David fits this description. He was immersed in God and fully alive!

David is the only man in Scripture described as "a man after God's own heart" (1 Samuel 13:14). It is the Godward heart of David that causes him to stand out. David got God's attention because of the heart he had developed—for God's unique use. One writer describes it by saying:

> The single most characteristic thing about David is God. David believed in God, thought about God, imagined God, addressed God, prayed to God. The largest part of David's existence wasn't David but God.[7]

It certainly wasn't his morality or ethics that were outstanding. David has nothing to teach us about success. His exploits in sin are notorious and controversial—from adultery and murder to his parenting style, he is anything but exemplary. David's passion for disobedience seems to match his wholehearted devotion in obedience. David is anything but passive.

Real Humanity

Why look at David? Is he a proper picture of manhood? Why not a more holy man of God like Joseph? Are there not better examples we could use? Of course there are. Far better examples than David abound if an almost-sinless existence is a picture of true manhood. But I don't think that's what manhood is all about. Eugene Peterson writes,

> The David story... presents us not with a polished ideal to which we aspire but with a rough-edged actuality in which we see humanity being formed—the God presence in the earth/human conditions. [8]

David, more than anyone else, shows us the aliveness of dealing with God in the human condition. It is this wholehearted man embracing life with vigor and danger that captures our view of masculinity. David deals with God and lets God deal with him.

True manhood is not about perfection, but about being a fully engaged human. A man who grapples with God, wrestles with uncertainty and fails, but also wins. In some way, David exemplifies all the qualities of being a wholehearted human—with both fiery devotion and unmitigated misjudgment—and yet he never quits. His whole life is the story of a man who continually cultivated his heart for God. He is the wholehearted man. He is the type of man with the type of heart that God is raising up today. He is what all men long to be.

Brené Brown, a qualitative researcher of sociology at the University of Houston, has written extensively on the subject of being wholehearted. She describes well-adjusted, joyful people as "living and loving with their whole heart. [9] She writes that such people are not the most talented, not the most successful, not even the most self-sufficient. She describes her journey of discovery in the realm of wholehearted living:

> The first word that came to mind [in my research] was wholehearted. I wasn't sure what it meant... I had a lot of questions about wholeheartedness. What did these folks value? As I started analyzing the stories and looking for re-occurring themes, I realized that the patterns generally fell into one of two columns; I first labeled these Do and Don't. The Do column was brimming with words like worthiness, rest, play, trust, faith, intuition, hope, belonging, joy, gratitude, and creativity. The Don't column was dripping with words like perfection, numbing, certainty, exhaustion, self-sufficiency, being cool, fitting in, judgment, and scarcity. [10]

Outside of Jesus Christ, I know of no other biblical figure that exemplifies the qualities above as much as David. Read his poetry (the Psalms) and you quickly pick up the sense of worthiness, trust, and hope that characterize this man. To watch his reaction as the Ark of the Covenant is brought into Jerusalem in 2 Samuel 6 is to experience pure, uninhibited joy and gratitude. David is the man we most should study if we long to be full-hearted and fully alive!

David didn't follow the rules, do everything right, "reach for the stars," or have a vision for his life! As a matter of fact, David doesn't fit our twenty-first-century leader or "good" Christian paradigms. He doesn't fit in, act cool, or follow what everyone tells him is proper protocol.

Why David? Because God is Who we need, and David wanted God; he hungered and thirsted for God above all else. David is our model because he is like all of us—full of dreams and passions misplaced; full of holy desires with a darkened heart. David is edgy, risky, and foolhardy. David is a living conundrum: a courageous coward.

Yet David is a man who aggressively went after God's heart. Despite his mistakes, he never gave up, never threw in the towel. He just kept getting up after each mistake. His capital was not his perfection but the direction of his heart. He was a battle-tested, wholehearted, forgiven sinner who was hungry for God and used for God's glory!

The Bloody Man

I believe it is just such humanity and wholehearted devotion that men need today. Our twenty-first-century Christianity is anything but zealous and wholehearted. Our twenty-first-century male is the child of The Sexual Revolution, a demasculinized culture, and quite frankly, a church where he doesn't fit. The professionalization of the clergy, boutique spirituality, slick churches, middle-class politeness, religious posturing, and what we might call "Mr. Rogers Christianity" is producing a nice, plastic, feminized, bourgeois Christian man who knows nothing of the bloody, wholehearted passion of a man like David.

We have been served a moralistic religiosity that is full of rigid positions, confusing requirements and a dumbed-down version of what truly matters to God. The Church is losing ground because we've lost the type of risk-taking, redemptive, foolish discipleship found in Scripture.

David is the wholehearted disciple who will fast and pray, worship all night, and take up his sling and fight a nine-foot giant. David is a man who will find himself utterly exhausted, get back up, and fight again and again and again. For him, all sin is forgivable, wrongs can be made right, and shame is overcome through authenticity. David is the picture of the kind of man all of us long to be.

I still remember the painting of David in the Children's Bible my mom read to me: There he is, standing in a valley, with a slight thrust of the hip. Tousled hair, six-pack abs, broad shoulders, a bulging forearm holding a dangling sling. Oh, and did I mention that he has one foot resting on the bloody, disarticulated head of a giant. That picture holds my attention. It did when I was eleven, and it does now.

This is the picture of a wholehearted man. Not the image we see on the flat screens in our dens, not the epicene actors we see portraying men as demasculinized wimps who always acquiesce to pressure. That's not wholehearted. Wholehearted is David rallying a disgruntled band of thieves, misfits, and eccentric outlaws into the greatest fighting force in all the Bible. In many ways, David is the prophetic picture of another Man who also rallied his band of nonconformists into an army that changed the world.

David points us to Jesus. David prepares us for the greatest wholehearted Warrior in human history. I have often found it intriguing that Jesus quotes David as He expires on the cross,

> *My God, My God, why have You forsaken Me?*
> *Why are You so far from helping Me,*
> *And from the words of My groaning?*
>
> *O My God, I cry in the daytime, but You do not hear;*
> *And in the night season, and am not silent.*
> **Psalm 22:1-2**

In Jesus' most helpless state, He calls upon the heartfelt words of David to describe His own heart. He identifies with the battles David fought and wrote about. Most commentators believe that Psalm 22, a poem of David, is a picture of the spiritual scene Jesus saw from the cross:

> *Many bulls have surrounded Me;*
> *Strong bulls of Bashan have encircled Me.*
>
> *They gape at Me with their mouths,*
> *Like a raging and roaring lion.*
>
> *I am poured out like water,*
> *And all My bones are out of joint;*
> *My heart is like wax;*
> *It has melted within Me.*
> **Psalm 22:12-14**

Jesus, "Son of David," is a man acquainted with grief and sorrow, not unlike David. Jesus lived it perfectly; David lived it like us. Jesus knew the poetry of David; his is the poem Jesus quotes. To be wholehearted is to love God with all our heart—even with the dark places, even with the sorrow, even alongside the brokenness and mistakes of our life. Wholeheartedness is loving with everything in our being—torn up, scarred, dejected—and yet hopeful and faithful. David prepares us for Jesus, and He is our model of Kingdom living,

> Jesus comes for sinners, for those outcast as tax collectors and for those caught up in squalid choices and failed dreams. He comes for corporate executives, street people, superstars, farmers, hookers,

addicts, IRS agents, AIDS victims, and even used-car salesman… His table fellowship with sinners will raise the eyebrows of religious bureaucrats… The Kingdom is not an exclusive, well-trimmed suburb with snobbish rules about who can live there. [11]

Other than Jesus, David is our model of a man who is fully alive, fully Kingdom-oriented, and fully human. A man with a broken but whole heart. Worshipper and warrior. Saint and sinner. Risky and dangerous. Full of fear and yet somehow, full of God!

David's heart, not religious posturing, is what we men need today. Wholehearted men. David, whose worship drives off demons. David, the warrior who subdues kingdoms. David, the sinner who cries out in repentance. David is the original worshipper and warrior—a type of man, a type of leader, a type of disciple—and yes, very dangerous.

The Dangerous Adventure: Day 1

1. **What word would best describe your Christian life right now? Why?**
   - o **Boring**
   - o **Dangerous**
   - o **Stuck**
   - o **Exciting**
   - o **Functional**
   - o **Passionate**
   - o **Complacent**
   - o **Moral**
   - o **Growing**

2. **Are you living the wholehearted life? Why or why not?**

3. **What do you hope to gain through this study of David?**

DAY 2: INTERVIEW

1 Samuel 13

11 And Samuel said, "What have you done?" Saul said, "When I saw that the people were scattered from me, and that you did not come within the days appointed, and that the Philistines gathered together at Michmash, 12 then I said, 'The Philistines will now come down on me at Gilgal, and I have not made supplication to the Lord.' Therefore I felt compelled, and offered a burnt offering."

13 And Samuel said to Saul, "You have done foolishly. You have not kept the commandment of the Lord your God, which He commanded you. For now the Lord would have established your kingdom over Israel forever. 14 But now your kingdom shall not continue. The Lord has sought for Himself a man after His own heart, and the Lord has commanded him to be commander over His people, because you have not kept what the Lord commanded you."

1 Samuel 16

If we do Not do what is right in the Lords eyes, we will lose everything

1 Now the Lord said to Samuel, "How long will you mourn for Saul, seeing I have rejected him from reigning over Israel? Fill your horn with oil, and go; I am sending you to Jesse the Bethlehemite. For I have provided Myself a king among his sons."

2 And Samuel said, "How can I go? If Saul hears it, he will kill me."
But the Lord said, "Take a heifer with you, and say, 'I have come to sacrifice to the Lord.' 3 Then invite Jesse to the sacrifice, and I will show you what you shall do; you shall anoint for Me the one I name to you."

4 So Samuel did what the Lord said, and went to Bethlehem. And the elders of the town trembled at his coming, and said, "Do you come peaceably?"

5 And he said, "Peaceably; I have come to sacrifice to the Lord. Sanctify yourselves, and come with me to the sacrifice." Then he consecrated Jesse and his sons, and invited them to the sacrifice.

6 So it was, when they came, that he looked at Eliab and said, "Surely the Lord's anointed is before Him!"

7 But the Lord said to Samuel, "Do not look at his appearance or at his

*physical stature, because I have refused him. For the Lord does not
see as man sees; for man looks at the outward appearance, but the
Lord looks at the heart."*

My wife and I have seven children. The older ones, now in their twenties, have all had job interviews. They've learned a few things from them, like "the first impression is the only first impression you will ever have."

So, they go out and purchase some new clothes and dress nicely. The outer appearance, the first look, is important in job interviews. My oldest son, a recent college graduate who is currently in the throes of looking for a job, said something interesting recently: "Dad, every day is a job interview. You never know who will be watching you." It's definitely true in his life. He was recently offered a job by a man in our church. This man had observed Daniel for months before talking to him. Daniel didn't know it, but he was being interviewed just by showing up to worship each week.

God does interviews every day. David had no idea, but God was interviewing him for a job he didn't even know about on the hills surrounding Bethlehem as he watched his father's sheep. God was conducting an interview with David as he fought a lion and a bear. As David stared into the heavens at night and penned yet another poem, God was gazing into his heart.

There was something about David's heart that caught God's attention. We have insight into the ways of the Lord through a seer who once came to a king and said, *"For the eyes of the LORD run to and fro throughout the whole earth, to show Himself strong on behalf of those whose heart is loyal to Him."* [12] God is constantly surveying the heart of men, looking across the earth for tender, bold, passionate hearts with which He can have an intimate relationship.

Getting God's Attention

God's ways of interviewing are not like those of man. God once interviewed Saul and found him to be a man humble enough to be king— but things had changed. Saul was too full of Saul—a master manipulator

(1 Samuel 13-16), a spinmeister. Saul had learned as king that he could fool all the people some of the time and some of the people all the time, but he had never discovered that he couldn't fool God *any* of the time. God saw the change in Saul's heart: Saul could not be trusted.

Samuel, the prophet who anointed Saul king, mourns the change in God's heart toward him. What he doesn't realize is that God is continuing his interview process.

> *God addressed Samuel: "So, how long are you going to mope over Saul? You know I've rejected him as king over Israel. Fill your flask with anointing oil and get going. I'm sending you to Jesse of Bethlehem. I've spotted the very king I want among his sons."*
> **1 Samuel 16:1-13 MSG**

God had "spotted the very king" he wanted because he had noticed the heart He had been searching for. God was interviewing David for the job of king. Samuel, the great prophet, had no clue. David was just being himself, but God saw something in him that set him apart. The Lord gives the prophet insight into what matters in His interview process,

> *But God told Samuel, "Looks aren't everything. Don't be impressed with his looks and stature. I've already eliminated him. God judges persons differently than humans do. Men and women look at the face; God looks into the heart."*
> **1 Samuel 16:7 MSG**

When my sons and daughters have job interviews, they go to the mall to purchase clothes. On the day of, they stare at the mirror. They make sure their hair isn't messed up when they walk in. But God isn't looking at the things man looks at—if He did, He never would have chosen David. After all, Saul had the height, the looks, the Ph.D. in being the first king of Israel (see 1 Samuel 9). The Bible says, "There was not a person more handsome in all of Israel."[13] But David had none of that. David didn't possess the outward appearance or attributes of Saul, but God's interview questions weren't focusing on those things.

Nobody involved in the drama in Bethlehem would have chosen David! Most scholars believe David was no more than fifteen years old at the time. (Some even say he was thirteen!) His brothers despised him (take note of Eliab in 1 Samuel 17:28), and to his father, he was only a keeper of the sheep. He was the youngest of eight sons and so dismissed that Jesse, his father, doesn't even remember him when Samuel shows up to interview his boys (see 1 Samuel 16:11, and an interesting cryptic note in Psalm 27:10).

Can you imagine? The greatest prophet in Israel has come to your humble home, invited your family to come along on a sacrifice, asking if he can interview your sons, and you forget one of them? Even Samuel has no idea that God has chosen David. He is ready to settle on Eliab because of his outward appearance (1 Samuel 16:7). David is insignificant even in his own family—but not to God!

God found David. He'd been interviewing him long before Samuel entered Jesse's home. David's heart and identity had caught God's attention. Asaph, the poet of Israel, would later write, "Then He chose David, His servant, hand-picked him from his work in the sheep pens ... His good heart made him a good shepherd."[14] God was interviewing David in the sheep pens when no one knew who he was.

An Actual Life

God is looking for men He can use for His purposes. David was simply being himself—not an ideal life, but an actual life; a life full of God. God isn't interested in and has never been impressed with outward appearance, education, skill, where we were born, who our father was, or what pedigree we possess.

The authentic life, the true self, the gritty inner heart of joy, pain, and passion are what characterize David. He is the authentic self. The "man after God's own heart" is a man who knows God's love and longs to know His passions. David will not live the perfectly designed, churchy life; David will not always make the wisest moral choices; David will be anything but a good father. But David has one thing many of us lack—he is authentic, real, and true to as much of himself as he knows at the time.

David would grow to understand the deep significance of the emotions and resolutions of the heart. More than one hundred times in his poetry, David references the heart. Through the hardships and betrayals he would experience, David would later write, "*The LORD is near to those who have a broken heart, and saves such as have a contrite spirit.*"[15] It was his most profound prayer that his heart would be right with God.

> *Let the words of my mouth and the meditation of my heart*
> *Be acceptable in Your sight,*
> *O Lord, my strength and my Redeemer.*
> **Psalm 19:14**

The Heart is Normally referring to the Mind

God interviewed David's heart, and he is interviewing ours. Like a divine stethoscope, Jesus listens to our heartbeat. God asks His questions at the heart level. God is always interviewing us through the motivations and intentions of our heart. God is wholehearted, and He is "spotting" the wholehearted. His crosshairs are on those who are wholeheartedly devoted to Him.

A Secret History with God

David developed a heart *for* God through a secret history *with* God. He was cut out of a different timber than Saul, a different timber than his brother Eliab. David had built a secret history of letting God build His heart into his own. David's heart had gradually become God's heart; God's heart had become David's. He was someone God could trust. He might have been one of the men Paul had in mind when he wrote to the church in Corinth,

we should never try to find ourselves we should let God build, and define us

> *I don't see many of "the brightest and the best" among you, not many influential, not many from high-society families. Isn't it obvious that God deliberately chose men and women that the culture overlooks and exploits and abuses, chose these "nobodies" to expose the hollow pretensions of the "somebodies"? ... Everything that we have—right thinking and right living, a clean slate and a fresh start—comes from God by way of Jesus Christ. That's why we have the saying, "If you're going to blow a horn, blow a trumpet for God."*
> **1 Corinthians 1:26–31 MSG**

27

God and David had a secret history of intimacy. We miss the whole point of the story if we think the encounter with Samuel was the first time David has heard a word from God. No, David has been chosen because this was *not* the first time! David had been tested by God long before Samuel showed up. Alan Redpath writes,

> The public anointing was the outcome of what had taken place in private between David and God long before. David was anointed for his great service and his ministry as Israel's king because God, who discerns the hearts of all men, knew that David's heart was different from others. He had prepared his heart.[16]

God's ability to use us, to trust us, is conditioned by our heart responses and motivations to His initiations when no one else sees or knows. David's life is a constant response to God with a God-aware heart. God is constantly inviting us into an intimate relationship of the heart. He is initiating time alone with us, so He might love us, speak to us, care for us, bless us, and minister to us. This is what God means in 2 Chronicles 16:9 about showing "Himself strong on behalf of those whose heart is loyal to Him."

God listens to the deepest strata of our souls—even in those places of pain, hurt, and self-hatred. David was no perfect soul; his later life will attest to that. He is a red-blooded man with ambitions and desires that are certainly less than holy. But what we observe is one who would have grasped the words of Isaiah and believed them:

> *I have summoned you by name; you are mine. When you pass through the waters, I will be with you ... Since you are precious and honored in my sight, and because I love you ... Though the mountains be shaken ... yet my unfailing love for you will not be shaken."*
> **Isaiah 42: 1,2,4; Isaiah 54:10 NIV**

It is God who calls us by name. The God who created the Grand Canyon, who formed the oceans, who gave us thunderstorms, lightning, and snow-capped mountains, knows our names! We are His and He is in us. He wants our hearts to worship Him and Him alone. A secret history of baring our hearts before Jesus, in the alone times, is the beginning of all masculinity.

The masculine heart is the heart that cries out for courage and strength in the context of shame and failure: "He teaches my hands to make war, so that my arms can bend a bow of bronze." It is in in the war-torn places of our heart that the authentic man finds he is beloved. It is in weariness that we discover the God-enriched life.

The interviews of God are at the heart level. God's not as interested in our outer lives as our inner responses. God's choice of a man is based on heart responses, not just head calculations. This is the walk of faith in the private life. This is difficult for most men—to look inward first and outward second. The work of God in a man, one who would become a worshipper and warrior, is based upon what God sees in "a heart response to His love." [17] God is longing for us to open our hearts to Him—the joys and even the deep, wounded places no one knows about; even those painful, shameful places we have hidden our whole lives. He already knows our hearts, but He so longs for us to let Him into the deeper recesses of our pain.

True Self

The road to intimacy with God begins with discerning our true selves. Brennan Manning once said, "The deepest desire of our hearts is for union with God." [18] It is when we surrender to our deeper heart's passion to seek after God that we can begin to come alive. Intimacy with Jesus is the deepest need of every man's heart. The true self is the authentic man who experiences and desperately wants intimate joy.

Recently I was on a retreat in the mountains of Colorado. I had been struggling with many questions about my future. As I began my prayer hike, I thought the quest of my soul was the church I was planting, and the next steps related to our discipleship ministry. As I climbed higher and higher into the forest, I unclothed my heart before God, sharing my struggles and failures.

A surprising thing happened: God spoke into my spirit these words, "Steve, I love *you* with all of *My* heart, all of *My* soul, and all of *My* strength." It was almost an audible voice! As the tears welled up and my body literally began to quake, I stopped and knelt down. Martin Lloyd-Jones wrote of "joy unspeakable;"[19] C.S. Lewis wrote, "I was surprised by joy ... everything else that had ever happened [was] insignificant in comparison."[20] In that moment, I knew exactly what they meant. I was filled with a sense of joy and acceptance. I knew at the heart level that I was beloved of God. My identity was not what I thought—the job of being a pastor—but rather my present belovedness in Christ.

Happiness and joy are not the same. The happiness of life is most often circumstantial, outward, and fleeting. But the joy of God is heart intimacy we nurture with God through the Holy Spirit in the alone times with Him. It is inner contact with God's heart. Our hearts beating with God's heart; this is the true self.

False Self

The battle for our hearts is with the false self that beats at the door of our minds, causing us to retreat into a life of false identity. The false self is the spiritual lethargy that creates anemic hearts that carry the cancer of half-hearted living. It is every man's struggle. It is the longing not for God and His joy, but a craving for attention and admiration. The false self of most men needs to brag, posture, position, and be the center of attention and respect. This has been me for to long

The false self-postures for attention because our heart isn't filled up. Every man's heart longs for a mission, a job to do, a vision to complete (more on this on Day Five). We men are wired that way. Yet, when we aren't experiencing intimacy with God, when our hearts are not filled with the love of God, we look to people, power, and position to fulfill our lives. It's the false self.

The false self is the loner who needs no one, who suffers nothing. He is "the lone ranger," the independent male of no loves, no needs, who always has what it takes. From the looks of this view today, it's not working. It's a farce, a ploy of Satan to kill our hearts. It is the false heart that leads to self-destruction.

It's the fig leaf of Adam. The false self is the uncovered dark place of our heart that we fear. We wear the fig leaf to cover up the shame of the false self, the imposter. And thus, we fill our life of falsity with a frenetic pace of activity and "success" that attempts to fill the loss of joy and peace. Thomas Merton writes,

> There is not substance under the things with which you are hollow and your structure of pleasure and ambitions has no foundation … When they are gone there will be nothing left of you but your own nakedness and emptiness and hollowness to tell you that you are your own mistake.[21]

And so, we wear the fig leaf of the false self because we fear the authenticity of the true self.

Intimacy Is the True You

Intimacy with Jesus is authenticity within ourselves. The true self is the authentic you. God wanted David and David wanted God. On that day in the mountains, God showed me His love. Not that I always love God with all my heart, though I certainly long to, but that He, the Lord and Creator of the universe, always loves me with all *His* heart! It was His heart love reaching out to me. Jesus opens His interview by sharing His heart with us,

> *This is how God showed his love for us: God sent his only Son into the world so we might live through him. This is the kind of love we are talking about—not that we once upon a time loved God, but that he loved us and sent his Son as a sacrifice to clear away our sins and the damage they've done to our relationship with God.*
> ***1 John 4:9-10 MSG***

The true self is the inward yes, the heart communion with a God who loves us. It is a heart response to God because He loves us "with all His heart, with all His soul, with all His strength." The interviews of God are the overtures of love from Him toward us and our responses to Him. It all began with His Son at Calvary, on the cross, and continues daily through a deepening love relationship.

The true self must learn to daily say no to the false self and yes to the interview of God, His love. It is through discovering authenticity and intimacy that we discover joy unspeakable and passion inexhaustible. David found it. And so can you and I.

Dive into Jesus today. Take a prayer walk, get alone, leave work early, don't rush into the next meeting, slow down. God is interviewing your heart and He waits for you to discover your true self. Take off the fig leaf and bear your heart to God. He already loves you. Receive His love.

The Dangerous Adventure: Day 2

1. **Pull away today into a lonely place, a quiet spot with no distractions, no noise and open your Bible to the most beloved of all passages of the Bible, Psalm 3. Read it three times and write down what God is saying to you.**

2. **How do you put on the fig leaf of the false self? In what ways do you struggle with boasting, posing, and pretending?**

3. **Share with the Lord your heart's desires. Make the following prayer your prayer right now to give yourself, the true self, to God:**

Father God, I thank You that You love me with all Your heart, with all Your soul, and with all Your strength. Thank you, Lord, that You showed Your love to me through sending Your Son, Jesus Christ, into the world to love and live through me. This is the kind of love I want—a love of truth, intimacy, and authenticity. Lord, I want to know You at the heart level. I want to have an intimate, personal, vital, growing relationship with You. Please come into my heart and give me a passion to know You at the deepest places of my heart. Amen.

DAY 3: OIL

Matthew 3
16 When He had been baptized, Jesus came up immediately from the water; and behold, the heavens were opened to Him, and He saw the Spirit of God descending like a dove and alighting upon Him.

Acts 1
8 "But you shall receive power when the Holy Spirit has come upon you; and you shall be witnesses to Me in Jerusalem, and in all Judea and Samaria, and to the end of the earth."

Acts 2
1 When the Day of Pentecost had fully come, they were all with one accord in one place. 2 And suddenly there came a sound from heaven, as of a rushing mighty wind, and it filled the whole house where they were sitting. 3 Then there appeared to them divided tongues, as of fire, and one sat upon each of them. 4 And they were all filled with the Holy Spirit.

1 Samuel 16
13 Then Samuel took the horn of oil and anointed him in the midst of his brothers; and the Spirit of the Lord came upon David from that day forward. So Samuel arose and went to Ramah.

For Jesus, it was like a dove descending from heaven as He stood dripping with the waters of the Jordan River (Matthew 3:16). For the disciples on the day of Pentecost, it was like wildfire falling from Heaven (Acts 2:3). For Paul, something like scales fell off his eyes (Acts 9:17-18). For David, the prophet Samuel stood before him, and *"took the horn of oil and anointed him in the midst of his brothers; and the Spirit of the LORD came upon David from that day forward."*[22] What's interesting, the words used for David's anointing sound strangely similar to the coming of the Holy

Spirit upon the disciples at Pentecost. Luke's description uses similar language, "when the Holy Spirit has come upon you."[23]

Throughout the Old Testament, the Holy Spirit is symbolized by oil. Appearing more than seventy times, the anointing of God, *mashach*, was a consecration with sacred oil upon persons and even places set apart for God's purposes (Exodus 30:25-29; 30:30; 40:9-14; Leviticus 8:12; 16:32, etc.). David is now being anointed with oil as a sign of being set apart to be the eventual king of Israel.

Anointing from God

At the end of his life, David recognized this anointing of oil as the coming of the Spirit. He writes of its significance in his last will and testament:

> *Now these are the last words of David.*
> *Thus says David the son of Jesse;*
> *Thus says the man raised up on high,*
> *The anointed of the God of Jacob,*
> *And the sweet psalmist of Israel:*
> *"The Spirit of the Lord spoke by me,*
> *And His word was on my tongue."*
> ***2 Samuel 23:1-2***

It is interesting that David begins his last testimony recorded in Scripture with a clear tip of his heart to the anointing of God as the empowerment of the Spirit. He is acknowledging that his poetic worship as "the sweet psalmist of Israel" is directly related to the anointing of God. The very words he spoke and wrote came from the Spirit of God. David, looking back over his life, begins his final prayer of praise with an understanding that the blessings of his life had come from the anointing of the Spirit.

Ethan, the writer of Psalm 89, would have agreed. Looking back, remembering the blessings of David and his anointed, Spirit-led leadership, he penned these words,

> *I have found My servant David;*
> *With My holy oil I have anointed him,*
> *With whom My hand shall be established;*

Also My arm shall strengthen him ...
"But My faithfulness and My mercy shall be with him,
And in My name his horn shall be exalted.
Psalm 89:20–24

Though David could not have known it at the time of his anointing, as young as he was, Samuel recognizes and records that the anointing with oil is the pouring out of the Holy Spirit upon David. David's whole life is about to change; his entire outlook is about to be transformed by God. Clearly, David is being set apart and called out on a mission. The young worshipper who loves the rolling hills of Bethlehem is about to be thrust into kingly halls of political strife and jealousy. The vibrant poet is soon to encounter a battlefield full of cowardice. The worshipper will become a warrior in an entirely new and challenging venue.

A Collision Course with Satan

God knows Davids heart because he made it.

We have talked about how God noticed David's heart, but now with the coming of the Spirit, Satan also notices him. David is on a collision course with a demonized king and there is a target on his back. It's not possible for a man chosen of God, set apart in the power of the Spirit, to be at peace with the devil. A man anointed of the Holy Spirit immediately becomes the target of Satan—the seed of the serpent and the seed of the woman will always be at enmity until Jesus comes.[24] David will need new power for new enemies. It is time to become a Spirit-filled man.

In Nigeria, it is customary for the men of a village to visit the home of a young boy to initiate him into manhood. Sometime between the ages of eleven and eighteen, the boy's father and the village elders crowd around his home. One man wearing a large mask over his head, along with a drummer, leads the group. The word for "mask" in Nigerian means "spirit." The masked/spirit man calls out from the group of men to the boy, "Come out, son of our people." One writer describes this scene by saying, "the masked man steps out first from among the men both to call the boy out and to usher him from the mother to the men; the spiritual dimension of manhood is understood from the outset as primary and essential."[25]

After several approaches to the boy, with the men chanting, "Come out!" the boy must leave his wailing mother at the door. It is interesting that neither the masked/spirit man nor any of the elders enter the boy's home, never crossing the threshold of the door, not pulling the boy out, never forcing the boy to join them. The boy is free to decide what he will do. For the Nigerian lad, life will never be the same. If he chooses to leave the safety and comfort of his mother and his home, he will enter the challenging and dangerous world of men. It's his moment of truth.

He will leave the village and be led out to the forest, where he will enter weeks of training with the older men. During this time, the boy will be circumcised and trained in hunting, construction, and the arts of his people. He will never live with his mother again, but rather live in his own thatched hut, built by his father. Upon the boy's return to the village, he's considered a man and his father hands him a gun and a hoe.[26] As a man, he must establish his way among the clan.

Called Out to Manhood

In a mystical, spiritual sense, David is also being called out to manhood through the anointing of the Holy Spirit. He is being called out by the national elder prophet, Samuel, to a new world—a world he never anticipated but for which he is ready. Before his family, before his father and brothers, possibly before the whole community of men—all can see the oil running down his head. It is an end to childhood and the beginning of manhood.

The Spirit of God being poured out upon him will empower him for the battles that lie ahead. His life is altered forever.

The Holy Spirit will give David supernatural courage against a foe who creates fear among trained warriors (1 Samuel 17:20-58). It will be from the anointing of the Spirit that David will learn to inquire and hear from God in distressing situations (1 Samuel 23-25). It will be from the Spirit of God that David will strengthen himself even when his closest allies are rejecting him (1 Samuel 30). David is changed into a new man with a new power through the anointing of the Holy Spirit.

Jesus, just before leaving the earth, clearly noting the inabilities, impulsiveness, and fears of his hand-selected men, instructed them not to do anything until they were filled with power from the Holy Spirit.

> *And being assembled together with them, He commanded them not to depart from Jerusalem, but to wait for the Promise of the Father, "which," He said, "you have heard from Me; for John truly baptized with water, but you shall be baptized with the Holy Spirit not many days from now."*
> ***Acts 1:4–5***

Even after three years of ministry together, even after being personally mentored by Jesus daily, still these men were not ready for the task of walking out their calling as men, as disciples, as worshippers and warriors, until they encountered the Holy Spirit. They are being thrust into a new world of persecution, demonic attacks, and obstacles they had never known before. They would need power for the work ahead. Pentecost would be their calling out as men into a mission.

Men, the Holy Spirit calls us out to manhood. It is the power of the Spirit that anoints, empowers, and lifts us into our calling as worshippers and warriors. Until we are filled with the Spirit we can never know our calling or our gifting. Until we are filled with the Spirit, we will never have the power (*dunamis* in Greek, the same root word for "dynamite") to live with wholehearted, passionate devotion.

The New Testament introduces us to the gifts of God, calling them the "gifts of the Holy Spirit." 1 Corinthians 12 and 14 and Romans 12 give us a glimpse into the gifts of God freely bestowed upon those who are filled with the Holy Spirit. These are not natural talents, skills, or abilities; they are sovereignly given and supernaturally bestowed upon the man who is filled with Spirit. Paul describes them as "the manifestation of the Spirit given to each one for the profit of all."[27] Clearly, we men cannot be all that God intended us to be without the anointing, the oil of the Spirit, upon our lives.

Without God's power, spiritual boys cannot become spiritual men God can mightily use. Without God's power, we cannot enter into being worshippers and warriors in Christ. Without power, one's Christian life will quickly burn out or fade away. The issue of power stands at the core of why most men cannot sustain their walk with God over the long haul. Even Jesus needed this anointing.

Clearly, Jesus needed power and received it in His baptism. He had never done a miracle, cast out a demon, preached a sermon, or healed a sick person until He was anointed with the Spirit (Matthew 4 and Luke 4). The disciples were not cleared to go out until they were filled with the Spirit. But once they were, they "turned the world upside down" (Acts 17:6) with their boldness and fierce devotion.

As men we will face issues in life that will demoralize, deflate, and defeat our passion for God. The array of God's enemies and their ways are found at every turn. Almost daily in my work as a pastor and teacher, I meet with men who are being bombarded by sexual temptations, financial limitations, and ethical complications. Without God's Spirit to give wisdom and guidance, their walk with God is soon compromised.

We must have the *dunamis* (dynamite) power of the Holy Spirit or we will crumble under the pressure. We must call out for the Holy Spirit to come upon us daily, that we might be men filled with God, who are fierce in our devotion and tender in our worship. The call today is for an advance of Spirit-baptized, bold, tenacious, tender men who love God, love their wives, love their children, and have homes built on the presence of God. This is only possible through surrender to the control of the Holy Spirit. A.W. Tozer once said, "Though all believers have the Spirit, the Spirit doesn't have all believers." How true! We may possess the Spirit when we are born again into Christ, but does the Spirit possess us?

To be filled and empowered with the Spirit of God is the only way we will be able to withstand the onslaught of the enemy. Even as demonic power is rising in these last days, so will the Lord baptize and empower

His Church with greater anointing.

As evil grows upon the earth, it is only through the Spirit of God that we can daily abide in Christ. John writes of the last days' deception and the need for abiding in the Spirit:

> *These things I have written to you concerning those who try to deceive you. But the anointing which you have received from Him abides in you ... as the same anointing teaches you concerning all things, and is true ... you will abide in Him. And now, little children, abide in Him, that when He appears, we may have confidence and not be ashamed before Him at His coming.*
> **I John 2; 26-28**

As a disciple of Christ, we have the Spirit living within our hearts; but it is this abiding in Christ, through God's power, that begins to build within us a God-confidence. Confidence in the Spirit, abiding in Christ, is the key to unashamed living. The Spirit desires to come in, fill us, and deliver us from shame. Confidence grows as we allow the anointing of the Spirit to rule over our hearts.

Power to Be Out of Control

In describing the coming of the Holy Spirit in Acts 2, one translation of the event at Pentecost reads, *"Then, like a wildfire, the Holy Spirit spread through their ranks."*[28]

I live in Black Forest, Colorado—a heavily forested area. A few years ago, we had a wildfire in our community that forced more than five thousand people to evacuate. Hundreds of homes were incinerated. The fire was burning just a quarter of a mile away from our house as we ran through it, grabbing stuff, packing it up in our trucks, and speeding down our road to safety. The combination of fifty-mile-an-hour winds coupled with bone-dry conditions turned our forest into a tinder box that created an inferno that blazed out of control for ten days.

Listen men: This is not unlike the Holy Spirit. The Spirit of God cannot be controlled, and He desires to burn through your heart.

One of the hardest things for a man is to let go and be willing to be out of control. Let's face it, in western Christianity, in our churches, at our jobs, being in control is not only helpful, it is required. But the reality of the stories and events of the men of the Bible is one of being controlled *by* the Spirit, which to our basic nature, often seems to be out of control. Spiritual manhood requires relinquishing control to the Spirit of God.

The Spirit of God is wild. Anyone who thinks they can control the Holy Spirit has no idea *Who* the Holy Spirit truly is. The ancient Celts may have come the closest to defining Him: The Celtic term for "Holy Spirit" was *An Geadh-Glas*, which translates as "the Wild Goose."[29] Celtic Christianity was one of the most vibrant and dynamic Christian movements in church history, reaching the Picts, Irish, Anglo-Saxons, and most of Europe. Their fierce boldness can be directly attributed to their understanding of the wild, powerful nature of the Holy Spirit. This belief vibrated through all they did. The most famous Celtic prayer, "St. Patrick's Breastplate," reads in part,

> I rise today in the power of Christ's birth and baptism,
> I rise today in the power of His crucifixion and burial,
> I rise today in the power of His rising and ascending,
> I rise today in the power of His descending and judging …
> I rise today with the power of God to pilot me,
> I rise today with God's strength to sustain me,
> I rise today with God's wisdom to guide me.[30]

The power to be out of our control but under God's control is not unlike a wildfire or a wild-goose chase. It is into this vibrant, robust, unpredictable adventure that the Holy Spirit calls us. A new manhood, a new calling, a new power, and a new chase—this is the calling out of the Spirit of God upon the man who is willing to be baptized and anointed by Him.

In writing to the Ephesians, Paul described the anointing of the Spirit: "And do not be drunk with wine, in which is dissipation; but be filled with

40

Being drunk makes us out of control, but the Spirit brings self-control the Spirit."[31] His audience was familiar with the religious sacrifices of the Temple of Artemis in that city; the Greeks believed that drunken orgies were the route to the spirit world. Paul is speaking of control. Instead of *what* is in control (alcohol), Paul is challenging the Ephesians to the question of *Who* is in control (Holy Spirit). Paul is metaphorically describing the need for us to be under the control of God through the filling of the Spirit.

To be called out by the Spirit Man (Christ Jesus) is to be called into a new life, a new anointing. The oil poured upon David, the dove lighting upon Jesus, and the wildfire falling upon the disciples all speak of the nature and loving power of the Spirit of God. He is calling you out; He desires that you and I would open our hearts to His wild and unpredictable power. Rather than living safe, caged lives, the chase for the wild goose is our invitation into a new manhood, a new outlook, and fresh adventure.

The Dangerous Adventure: Day 3

1. **Are you willing to let the Spirit of God have control over your life? If so, what areas of your life are currently *not* under His control?**

2. **Now give to the Lord these area(s) and allow Him to anoint you with the oil of His Spirit. A sample prayer:**

Lord Jesus, I confess that I have been in control of my life. I confess that I have not trusted You or walked with You in the full power of Your Spirit. I ask you to take control of _____ and fill me with Your Spirit. I cannot live out my manhood without Your power. Come, Holy Spirit, and fill me with Your love, Your power, and Your presence. Anoint me for the adventure that lies ahead. I am available for your purposes. Amen.

3. **God is calling you out into a new Spirit-empowered manhood. Your whole life is gradually changing. Make a list of the ways you want God to transform your life in the days ahead.**

DAY 4: WORSHIPPER

1 Samuel 16

14 But the Spirit of the Lord departed from Saul, and a distressing spirit from the Lord troubled him. 15 And Saul's servants said to him, "Surely, a distressing spirit from God is troubling you. 16 Let our master now command your servants, who are before you, to seek out a man who is a skillful player on the harp. And it shall be that he will play it with his hand when the distressing spirit from God is upon you, and you shall be well."

17 So Saul said to his servants, "Provide me now a man who can play well, and bring him to me."

18 Then one of the servants answered and said, "Look, I have seen a son of Jesse the Bethlehemite, who is skillful in playing, a mighty man of valor, a man of war, prudent in speech, and a handsome person; and the Lord is with him."

19 Therefore Saul sent messengers to Jesse, and said, "Send me your son David, who is with the sheep." 20 And Jesse took a donkey loaded with bread, a skin of wine, and a young goat, and sent them by his son David to Saul. 21 So David came to Saul and stood before him. And he loved him greatly, and he became his armorbearer. 22 Then Saul sent to Jesse, saying, "Please let David stand before me, for he has found favor in my sight." 23 And so it was, whenever the spirit from God was upon Saul, that David would take a harp and play it with his hand. Then Saul would become refreshed and well, and the distressing spirit would depart from him.

It was hot, humid, and sultry from a monsoon rain. Sweat poured down my face and back. The downpour had lasted less than an hour, but the streets were flooded, and traffic was at a standstill. The sound of singing—passionate, loud, exuberant praise—could be heard through the crowded streets as I jumped off the jeep taxi and walked into Jesus Tabernacle.

WORSHIPPER WARRIOR

This was Manila, Philippines, and I was entering a dilapidated tin-roofed barn, filled to capacity with the most joyful people I had ever met. Smiling faces, uplifted hands, and flaming hearts—men, women, and children celebrating the love of Christ with one single passion. There was no electricity (thank God, since we were standing in six inches of water) and no praise band, but everyone in the room was fixed on the beauty and name of Jesus through simple choruses and upturned hearts. Jesus' Tabernacle may not have had electrical power, but it had Jesus power! The manifest presence of Jesus filled the room.

Worship is not about songs or cool, performance-driven bands, but about Jesus. We have often been guilty of viewing worship as primarily the singing of music in a church setting. In our American churches, we define worship more based on skill and gifting than about the heart of the worshipper and the presence of Jesus.

It was no different three thousand years ago. David, the shepherd boy from Bethlehem, is noticed by Saul and his court because they've heard about the effect of his harp, not the depth of his heart. They notice the skill of his playing but overlook the passion of his life.

> *"Let our master now command your servants, who are before you, to seek out a man who is a skillful player on the harp. And it shall be that he will play it with his hand when the distressing spirit from God is upon you, and you shall be well."*
>
> *So Saul said to his servants, "Provide me now a man who can play well, and bring him to me."*
>
> *Then one of the servants answered and said, "Look, I have seen a son of Jesse the Bethlehemite, who is skillful in playing ... and the Lord is with him."*
> **1 Samuel 16:16–18**

Saul wants a man who can play the harp well. Maybe this is his favorite instrument. He wants good, solid music for his court. He wants a personal concert with a gifted musician. But something's afoot in God's plan; take notice that there is an astute servant, a true worshipper, in Saul's court. Within Saul's entourage, God has placed one with an observant heart. The last sentence is the cryptic secret to David's success: This servant who will remain obscure says, "and the Lord is with him." The presence of God is with David! Saul can't see it, but God and a lone servant do.

The Gaze

The presence of God is *with* David because he is a worshipper. David has invited the presence of God into all he does, even playing the harp. His outward skill is only a reflection of the intimacy of his heart in worship. Saul's men notice the skill, the music, and its effect—but God notices David because of his heart in worship.

David is foremost a worshipper. David's gaze is upon God.

David has the presence of God over his life in all he does, not just in playing music. David is walking daily in the presence of God because his life is devoted to God in all he does. He has a lifestyle of worship, not just skill in playing a musical instrument. God's presence was upon David because David's gaze was upon God. Tim Hughes, one of the great worship leaders of our time, has said, "The first thing God calls us to do is to watch Him—to gaze into His eyes and behold His greatness."[32] The first thing in David's life is this preoccupation with gazing at God. David, in one of his poems, expresses well his foremost passion as a worshipper:

> *One thing I have desired of the Lord,*
> *That will I seek:*
> *That I may dwell in the house of the Lord*
> *All the days of my life,*
> *To behold the beauty of the Lord,*
> *And to inquire in His temple.*
> **Psalm 27:4**

David is saying the most important thing in his life, the most effective thing he could do, was gaze upon the beauty of God and seek after Him. David's desire to seek the Lord, to be in the presence of God, was the one controlling passion of his life. All the days of his life, every day afforded to him, David wanted his one great overriding ambition to be gazing upon the beauty of the Lord.

The Manifest Presence

David's gaze, his passion, his one desire is God. God is what David is about. Not money, not position, not power. David is about God and thus, God is about David. God hangs out with men who like hanging out with Him. Though God is everywhere (omnipresent), He is not everywhere manifested. Where God is uplifted, God will manifest Himself. And where God is manifested, His power shows up. Watch what happens next in David's journey.

> *And so it was, whenever the spirit from God was upon Saul, that David would take a harp and play it with his hand. Then Saul would become refreshed and well, and the distressing spirit would depart from him.*
> **1 Samuel 16:23**

David's worship is driving back demons! David is the first exorcist in the Bible! The distressing spirit over Saul seems to be demonic, and it is clearly the life and worship David brings that refreshes Saul. David is a wholehearted worshipper, and his worship ushers in the presence and power of God, which pushes back darkness. Might this be the very essence of what C.S. Lewis discovered as he studied David's poetry, the Psalms, when he wrote "it is in the process of being worshiped that God communicates his presence to men."[33] And it is in His manifest presence through the wholehearted David that darkness is shoved back!

A lifestyle of worship and praise is a life that invites the manifest presence of God. Worship is where God is the most comfortable. David, understanding this, would later write, "Thou inhabits the praises of Israel" (Psalm 22:3). Worship brings God. Worship is where God lives. It is God's permanent address.[34] God is most at home in worship, and His favor most abides with those who walk in such worship.

Simultaneously, where God is most at home, Satan is most displaced. God's home, Heaven, is one perpetual worship service. Revelation 4 gives us a glimpse into the heavenly realm of God's most comfortable dwelling place—a sanctuary of constant, twenty-four/seven praise and worship. Satan and sin can't dwell there. God's home, the place where He has complete control, has no darkness within it. Satan was driven out of Heaven (Revelation 12) and has been cast upon the earth. Praise and worship continue the process of driving out the enemy of our souls.

God's Design

Yet we live lives that are anything but worshipful. Rather than a passionate pursuit after God, we are often tempted to allow our hearts to worship at the altar of ambition, power, and success. We have been lied to by the enemy and our culture, believing that it is through such a life that happiness can be found. Under such a lie, our hearts shrivel up and our zeal for God dies.

So much of our lives as men are spent in an endless drive to succeed. The ambition of our lives is the pursuit of happiness through getting ahead in business and making the corporate bottom line each quarter. We are obsessed with competitive sales performances and getting that next promotion. And in the meantime, our hearts are dying.

Our hearts were designed by the Lord to gaze upon Him. Our hearts come alive with worship—even the wrong kind of worship. You can especially see the worshipper's heart when a group of men get together to talk sports. I live in Colorado and during football season, the conversation among every male from September to January (February if they make the Super Bowl) is the Denver Broncos. Whether they are having a winning or losing season makes no difference; we talk Broncos constantly. And if there's a major victory or upset, the men praise and excitedly recount the plays that won the game. We worship at the altar of the Denver Broncos every fall. C.S. Lewis came to understand this aspect of our natural desire for praise.

> The world rings with praise—lovers praising their mistresses [Romeo praising Juliet and vice versa], readers their favourite poet, walkers praising the countryside, players praising their favourite game—praise of weather, wines, dishes, actors, motors, horses, colleges, countries, historical personages, children, flowers, mountains, rare stamps, rare beetles, even sometimes politicians or scholars... praise almost seems to be inner health made audible. ... just as men spontaneously praise

whatever they value, so they spontaneously urge us to join them in praising it: "Isn't she lovely? Wasn't it glorious? Don't you think that magnificent?"[35]

We all worship. Our hearts were created for worship. Worship is the gaze, the focus, the preoccupation with something. From our first hit in Little League to our first car, we naturally gush over that which we value. We were born for praise and worship because our heart longs to be captured by something or someone greater and more magnificent than ourselves. The question is not will we worship, but rather who or what will we worship?

The Apostle Paul understood God designed us for worship. Paul had grown up in a devout Jewish home. As a young man, he was trained in the Harvard of the Middle East under the greatest of Hebrew teachers, Gamaliel. Paul called himself a Hebrew of Hebrews, zealous for the traditions of his forefathers (Philippians 3). He had grown up around the Jewish temple ritual as the means of worship, a system built on the sacrifices of animals. Thus, upon his spiritual rebirth (Acts 9) and experience of intimacy with Jesus, he would use the language of the Jewish sacrificial system in expressing a new kind of worship:

> *I beseech you therefore, brethren, by the mercies of God, that you present your bodies a living sacrifice, holy, acceptable to God, which is your reasonable service. And do not be conformed to this world, but be transformed by the renewing of your mind, that you may prove what is that good and acceptable and perfect will of God.*
> ***Romans 12:1-2***

Rather than a sacrifice of animals, Paul speaks of the sacrifice of everything in our lives as a new form of worship. Our lives are to be as living sacrifices. Not the dead sacrifices of an old order, the old covenant and ritual of the Jewish system, but rather a new kind of worship, a new way of relating to God—a living way, a lively way, a daily way.

Our worship is the surrender of our lives upon the stone altar of life before God. The way of this world and the values of this world will lead to death. The ambition for success and the accumulation of things as our primary focus only leads to the death of our hearts. This is the worship of the world. But Paul is inviting us to a new living sacrificial system—an engagement of our whole being, our whole heart. This is a living sacrifice! Our hearts can come alive, and the living heartbeat of our existence can be a sacrificial surrender to the God who has given us life!

This is the new life, the normal life, the life of praise and worship—presenting our bodies to Christ. This is the design of God, that we would daily give our hearts, passions, desires, loves, frustrations, concerns, up to God on the altar of worship. This is not radical but normal. For this is the very essence of what you were called to do. But it cannot happen without a new heart, a heart designed by God for worship.

The Heart of Worship

We have seen that through the depth of David's heart, he is a wholehearted, passionate seeker after God. He has a heart that is in tune with God's heart, that runs after God. The Bible has more to say about the heart than any other topic. John Eldredge explains,

> The subject of the heart is addressed in the Bible more than any other topic—more than works or service, more than belief or obedience, more than money ... Maybe God knows something we've forgotten.[36]

And indeed, we have forgotten. We have become machines and robots to our world system and have forgotten the deep longings of our hearts. Intimacy with God is seeking God with all our heart. "You will find Me," God says, "when you seek Me with all of your heart" (Jeremiah 29:13). Jesus, in expressing the greatest of all commandments and arguably the essence of worship, said,

> *"'And you shall love the Lord your God with all your heart, with all your soul, with all your mind, and with all your strength.' This is the first commandment. And the second, like it, is this: 'You shall love your neighbor as yourself.' There is no other commandment greater than these."*
> **Mark 12:30-31**

A lifestyle of worship, the reasonable worship, is a life of loving God with our entire being—our heart, our soul, our mind, and our strength. And then as a result, loving our neighbor as ourselves. Do this, Jesus says, and you will find your purpose, the purpose for your existence. It's all here. This is the heart of worship. It is from the heart that we give ourselves to God as a living sacrifice. "The heart is the connecting point, the meeting place between any two persons."[37] And it is at the heart level that we encounter God. This can happen anytime, anyplace, within any context. God manifests His presence when our hearts are engaged with His being.

How is your heart today? Worship begins with surrender to the only One worthy of worship—Jesus Christ. This is not just a one-time decision but a wholehearted, daily experience with Christ. We can only worship One with Whom we have a connection at the heart level. He loves you and has His gaze upon you. Jesus longs to connect daily through a relationship of intimacy. This is the true meaning of worship.

A New Heart

Paul wrote that upon our surrender to Him, "Christ [will] dwell in your heart through faith" (Ephesians 3:17). Christ can only dwell in a heart that has been restored and transformed by His Spirit. When you give your old heart to Christ, when you repent of the idols you worshipped, He comes in and restores you with a new heart, recreated by God for worship—a heart that is hungering for sacrificial worship.

> *I will give you a new heart and put a new spirit within you; I will take the heart of stone out of your flesh and give you a heart of flesh. I will put My Spirit within you and cause you to walk in My statutes, and you will keep My judgments and do them.*
> ***Ezekiel 36:26-27***

God gives you a new heart when you surrender to Him. If you are a Jesus disciple, you have a new heart. Your sinful heart is transformed into a good heart, a worshipping heart that creates new passions, new desires, and a new vision to walk in the ways of the Lord! Now, that is something to jump up and shout about. You have a new heart!

John Eldredge captures this perspective, writing, "We have new hearts.

Do you know what this means? Your heart is good. Let that sink in for a moment. Your heart is good … Those of you who have gotten your hearts back know exactly what I mean. It's freedom. It's life."[38] I would add that it's the life of a worshipper. David had it, and it's available to all of us. The life of worship comes forth as we engage our hearts—our new hearts, our hearts of flesh—into a gaze and love for God. This is what you were created for, to become a worshipper. Worship springs forth from our new heart.

We have a good heart, so we can now say yes to God, give our bodies to Christ, focus our attention upon Jesus daily. The presence of God will be upon us as we practice worship in every endeavor each day. This kind of worship drives back darkness and presses out demonic powers. This is what David had that Saul missed, but a servant of the court understood. The Spirit of the Lord was upon David. The Spirit of the Lord can also be upon us.

So now is the time to enter the adventure of worship. Becoming a worshipper of God is what your new heart was created for. The presence of God will begin to characterize your work, your play, your essence. What could be more powerful and more heartfelt than that?

The Dangerous Adventure: Day 4

1. **Does God have your whole heart? If not, what are the idols or hindrances of your life that block wholehearted worship? Make a list of those things that occupy the center of your life:**

2. Now, surrender each of those idols up to Christ, and ask the Lord to transform you by giving you a heart for Him. Use this prayer to help in giving your life to Christ:

Lord Jesus, I want to be a worshipper of You and You only. I recognize that I have idols in my life that occupy my heart. I give you my worship of _____ and I invite You to come in and transform my heart. I want You to rule and reign in my heart from this day forward. Forgive me. Transform me. Empower me with Your Spirit and guide me into the new heart that You've given me. I want to begin to love You with my whole heart, my whole body, my entire being. Make me into a worshipper of You and only You. Amen.

3. Begin this day by worshipping the Lord. Look up the song "Amazing Grace" by Chris Tomlin on YouTube and sing along. Let God speak to your heart as you sing.

DAY 5: CAUSE

1 Samuel 17

4 And a champion went out from the camp of the Philistines, named Goliath, from Gath, whose height was six cubits and a span. 5 He had a bronze helmet on his head, and he was armed with a coat of mail, and the weight of the coat was five thousand shekels of bronze. 6 And he had bronze armor on his legs and a bronze javelin between his shoulders. 7 Now the staff of his spear was like a weaver's beam, and his iron spearhead weighed six hundred shekels; and a shield-bearer went before him. 8 Then he stood and cried out to the armies of Israel, and said to them, "Why have you come out to line up for battle? Am I not a Philistine, and you the servants of Saul? Choose a man for yourselves, and let him come down to me. 9 If he is able to fight with me and kill me, then we will be your servants. But if I prevail against him and kill him, then you shall be our servants and serve us." 10 And the Philistine said, "I defy the armies of Israel this day; give me a man, that we may fight together." 11 When Saul and all Israel heard these words of the Philistine, they were dismayed and greatly afraid.

12 Now David was the son of that Ephrathite of Bethlehem Judah, whose name was Jesse, and who had eight sons. And the man was old, advanced in years, in the days of Saul. 13 The three oldest sons of Jesse had gone to follow Saul to the battle. The names of his three sons who went to the battle were Eliab the firstborn, next to him Abinadab, and the third Shammah. 14 David was the youngest. And the three oldest followed Saul. 15 But David occasionally went and returned from Saul to feed his father's sheep at Bethlehem.

16 And the Philistine drew near and presented himself forty days, morning and evening.

17 Then Jesse said to his son David, "Take now for your brothers an ephah of this dried grain and these ten loaves, and run to your brothers at the camp. 18 And carry these ten cheeses to the captain of their thousand, and see how your brothers fare, and bring back news of them." 19 Now Saul and they and all the men of Israel were in the Valley of Elah, fighting with the Philistines.

20 So David rose early in the morning, left the sheep with a keeper, and took the things and went as Jesse had commanded him. And he came to the camp as the army was going out to the fight and shouting for the battle. 21 For Israel and the Philistines had drawn up in battle array, army against army. 22 And David left his supplies in the hand of the supply keeper, ran to the army, and came and greeted his brothers. 23 Then as he talked with them, there was the champion, the Philistine of Gath, Goliath by name, coming up from the armies of the Philistines; and he spoke according to the same words. So David heard them. 24 And all the men of Israel, when they saw the man, fled from him and were dreadfully afraid. 25 So the men of Israel said, "Have you seen this man who has come up? Surely he has come up to defy Israel; and it shall be that the man who kills him the king will enrich with great riches, will give him his daughter, and give his father's house exemption from taxes in Israel."

26 Then David spoke to the men who stood by him, saying, "What shall be done for the man who kills this Philistine and takes away the reproach from Israel? For who is this uncircumcised Philistine, that he should defy the armies of the living God?"

27 And the people answered him in this manner, saying, "So shall it be done for the man who kills him."

28 Now Eliab his oldest brother heard when he spoke to the men; and Eliab's anger was aroused against David, and he said, "Why did you come down here? And with whom have you left those few sheep in the wilderness? I know your pride and the insolence of your heart, for you have come down to see the battle."

29 And David said, "What have I done now? Is there not a cause?" 30 Then he turned from him toward another and said the same thing; and these people answered him as the first ones did.

Just a few blocks away from London's Westminster Abbey, between St. James Park and Parliament Square, I finally found Clive Steps on King Charles Street. I descended the old stone steps well below the city streets and entered an austere concrete bunker. Light bulbs hung from wires, maps of Europe covered the walls, and different-colored rotary phones littered the desks scattered around the room. It was exactly as it had been more than sixty years ago—damp and cold, the same as it was in those dark days in 1940. These were the British government's war rooms during the Nazi bombing of London in the summer and autumn of that year. I had come to see where a man who many considered a failure had become a man transformed.

Winston Spencer Churchill spent the majority of his adult life in politics, following in his father's footsteps. He had once been considered a rising star, but as the years had passed he was all but forgotten. His many mistakes and miscalculations had mounted. He was often considered inept, impetuous, out of step with the times, and most of all, unwilling to listen to reasonable men. By the 1930s, he had become an outlaw in the House of Commons.

Even as Adolf Hitler and Germany's Third Reich rose in military power, all the major nations in Europe, influenced strongly by British Prime Minister Neville Chamberlain, only wanted peace. With more than thirty-seven million casualties less than two decades before, memories of the carnage of World War I ran long and deep in the hearts of Europeans. The "war to end all wars" had been the soil that gave rise to a new breed of politicians: men who would do virtually anything, even compromising principle, to avoid war. The Roaring Twenties, the League of Nations, and new international treaties had fueled visions of lasting peace.

Churchill was out of step with the social and political times. He hated what was happening and despised the pacifist policies of England and France. He railed against the peace-at-all-costs social and political status quo; very few cared for the old man's rhetoric.

As the years passed, Churchill spent his days writing, building ponds and walls at his home, and painting. His speeches in the House of Commons decrying Hitler and rising fascism in Europe were often heard by less than a dozen backbenchers. Lady Astor, a leading lady of England, upon being asked about Churchill, replied, "Oh, he's finished."[39] Mocked in the press[40] and shouted down by students at Edinburgh University,[41] his political career seemed doomed. A book about his waning career was even published in 1931—*The Tragedy of Winston Churchill.*[42]

But as the Nazi war machine gained strength, as nation after nation was enslaved, all of Europe was engulfed in war. On May 10, 1940, "*The Last Lion*" (the title of the famous three-volume work on Churchill by William Manchester) became the top leader of England. With Chamberlain's ignominious resignation, Churchill became prime minister. He was sixty-five years old.

With all of Western Europe now in his bloodthirsty, sadistic clutches, Hitler set his sights on taking over England. What he hadn't bargained on were the lionhearted convictions of Winston Churchill. On July 14, 1940, in a BBC broadcast, Churchill spelled out his beliefs:

> This is no war of chieftains or of princes, of dynasties or national ambition; it is a war of peoples and of causes. There are vast numbers, not only in this island but in every land, who will render faithful service in this war, but whose names will never be known, whose deeds will never be recorded. This is a War of the Unknown Warriors; but let all strive without failing in faith or in duty, and the dark curse of Hitler will be lifted from our age.[43]

Churchill would later be hailed as one of the most influential leaders of the twentieth century. In 1940 and 1949, Churchill was *Time* magazine's Man of the Year. He would later write of his bulldog mentality and love of a cause worth fighting for by saying,

> Never give in—never, never, never, never, in nothing great or small, large or petty, never give in except to convictions of honour and good sense. Never yield to force; never yield to the apparently overwhelming might of the enemy.[44]

God most often uses unknown, forsaken warriors for His purposes. God plants His cause in the hearts of men to fight His battles on the earth.

David, the lionhearted, was just such a man. Unknown to men but known to God, David's heart was being prepared for a cause worth fighting for.

The Valley

Forty days had passed in the Valley of Elah (1 Samuel 17). As all of Israel and all of Philistia faced off to determine who would rule the land, the nine-foot-tall Goliath from Gath—who many scholars believe was a descendant of the Anakin, giants of men who once occupied the region (Genesis 14; Joshua 11)—would come out into the valley and challenge the Israeli army. Samuel records the famous story.

> *Then [Goliath] stood and cried out to the armies of Israel, and said to them, "Why have you come out to line up for battle? Am I not a Philistine, and you the servants of Saul? Choose a man for yourselves, and let him come down to me. If he is able to fight with me and kill me, then we will be your servants. But if I prevail against him and kill him, then you shall be our servants and serve us." And the Philistine said, "I defy the armies of Israel this day; give me a man, that we may fight together."*
> **1 Samuel 17:8–10**

Goliath's challenge is for a man, a warrior! "Give me a man" to fight, he bellows. The battle will be for a man, just one man. Is there not a man who will fight? This is the valley David enters, a valley with only one warrior—Goliath.

This was a common battle strategy in ancient times. It was known as "single combat." To save both armies the bloodshed of open combat, they would choose just one man from each side to fight. One victorious fighter could secure the destiny of a nation. Goliath threw down the gauntlet—one warrior, one fight, one victor.

It's been forty days of this same boastful speech by Goliath. Yet no one moves. Fear hangs like a morning fog over the Valley of Elah. David, bringing food to his three eldest brothers, hears the challenge for the first time. His heart is moved. He responds differently than his brothers—differently than even the king of Israel, Saul.

David's heart is out of step with the other men of Israel. His is not conditioned by peace, safety, and security: David's heart is conditioned by a secret history with God in the hills of Bethlehem. David, an unknown warrior with a burning passion for the glory and love of God—a deep, wholehearted human—sizes up the challenge differently than those around him.

A Reasonable Faith

Upon hearing the challenge, David begins to ask about the meaning of Goliath's prideful, blasphemous words. David's older brother, Eliab—possibly jealous, certainly miscalculating—counters David's questions by suggesting he only wants the thrill of watching a battle.

> *Now Eliab his oldest brother heard when he spoke to the men; and Eliab's anger was aroused against David, and he said, "Why did you come down here? And with whom have you left those few sheep in the wilderness? I know your pride and the insolence of your heart, for you have come down to see the battle."*
> **1 Samuel 17:28**

David's response is telling. "What have I done now? *Is there* not a cause?"[45] David uses an interesting Hebrew word for "cause." The word literally means, "reasonable grounds for a belief or action."[46] For David, with a heart conditioned by the intimate interviews of God, conditioned on the lonely hills of Bethlehem with lyre in hand and praise upon his lips, this is only a reasonable question.

David is offended and angered by Goliath's defiant tone. His heart is being torn apart by the pride and insolence of this idol-worshipping soldier. He essentially is saying, "Is there not a reasonable faith to believe that the glory of God is a cause worth fighting for?"

David's question seems entirely sensible to him, but insensible—even foolish—to his brother. Saul will concur with Eliab. But David's reasoning powers had been forged with God, not with men. David's imagination had been hewn out of the timber of a worshipper's heart. His spirit had been born out of intimacy with God in the hills around Bethlehem, not in the Valley of Elah. Up to this point, the valleys of David's life had been full of God. But this valley was different.

God-Sized Imagination

The battle is always for a man who can fight—for a man with God-filled imagination. David has entered a valley with a Goliath-sized imagination.[47] In the Valley of Elah stands an army of men who are overwhelmed, saturated with, and dominated through and through by Goliath. David's question about a cause worth fighting for is treated with disrespect and contempt. Eugene Peterson captures the situation well: "The same debased imagination that treated Goliath as important treated David as insignificant. The men who were in awe of Goliath were contemptuous of David."[48] The thinking in the valley that day was full of fear and intimidation.

Goliath-dominated imagination never sees the opportunities of faith. For those who are marked by it, the question is, "How can we just survive the situation?" David, who has fought lions and bears while watching his sheep, has a God-sized imagination. He is dominated by an imagination built up through faith and trust, not fear and survival. Through a secret history of prayer, meditation, worship, and a God-saturated imagination, David comes upon a scene that is an affront to his heart. God's power and glory are at stake. David sees it all as a cause worth fighting for, even dying for.

As David has been tending sheep, God has been interviewing David's heart, preparing him for a Goliath-sized challenge. The Psalms show David's imagination, developed through a focus on the majesty of God. In worship and prayer, through taking on the challenges of protecting his sheep, David has an imagination that can feel what God feels. It is when we feel what God feels that we are most prepared to do what God does.

Someone has said faith is to God what fear is to Satan. The moment we allow fear to dominate our thinking is the moment we lose our imagination. Saul's men had no imagination of God because they were overrun with Goliath-sized fears. David had not lost his heart or his God-sized imagination. David's heart was still tender. He could feel that

Goliath's accusations were wrong and God-defying. His whole heart was touched by the wrongness of the challenge and the rightness of God's cause.

Men, you were created for a cause worth fighting for, a cause worth dying for. You were made for impact. At the very essence of our manly humanity is a passion for a cause. It is the reason we flock to movies like *Braveheart, Lord of the Rings,* and *American Sniper*. We see in these men something we long for—the cause of fighting for something more majestic than mere existence. It is the core of wholeheartedness. God made our hearts to be filled up with His cause, His mission.

Pandemic of the Heart

Yet we as men are filled with anything but the cause of God. We have a pandemic of the heart. Ebola and other medical epidemics have dominated the news over the past few years. Every major news outlet has reported the danger of such diseases and viruses. But of greater danger than any physical pandemic is the spiritual disease of Goliath-saturated thinking that warps our minds and atrophies our hearts. We have spiritual Ebola.

Our lives have become anything but a cause worth dying for. Our lives consist of freeze-dried, zip-locked, low-calorie, pre-packaged busyness that saturates our thinking. From worries about the scratch on our new car to how well the stock market is performing, we have replaced our swords with cell phones. The disease of the mundane is pandemic with us men, and it's killing our hearts.

We are the consumers of the information age, computers, and twenty-four/seven news cycles that force us to constantly stare at our cell phones. Even my phone has an app for measuring the carbs I eat at each meal—and as if that wasn't enough information, it also computes how many pounds of fat I will accrue as a result. (I'm over fifty and I'll be honest—that's too much information!)

Our culture bombards us with mixed messages about our purpose as men. John Eldredge writes,

> Society at large can't make up its mind about men. Having spent the last thirty years refining masculinity into something more sensitive, safe, manageable and, well, feminine, it now berates men for not being men… "Where are all the real men?" is regular fare for talk shows and new books. You asked them to be women, I want to say. The result is a gender confusion never experienced at such a wide level in the history of the world.[49]

It's a spiritual virus. But our hearts were made for a cause greater than ourselves. We long to make an impact upon others. We were designed by God for a cause. Years ago, I heard a missionary say, "If it's not worth dying for, it's not worth living for." Our hearts come alive with a purpose that calls us out of our self-imposed boredom into the adventure of the Kingdom of God. The cause of Christ is what makes our hearts come alive.

Man on a Mission

If you were to read about Jesus in most publications today, you would get the impression that He was a good-natured, loving, wanderlust minstrel who showed up at parties and weddings, multiplied the beer, did some healings, and hitchhiked to the next town.

I grew up in the church. I was in church nine months before I was born. My dad was a pastor. The image of Jesus given to me in Sunday School was a California surfer with a beard—cool, laid-back, digs everyone, and is generous to all. No offense offered, none taken.

Yet, the Bible paints a different image. The Bible frames Jesus more in the spirit of a freedom fighter, an activist, an outlaw, than some cool, laid-back beachcomber.

Jesus is not wandering around, but rather a man who is clearly taking His marching orders from His Heavenly Father. Jesus is a man with a cause; a man on a mission. In the first days of his public ministry, Jesus spells out His purpose on the earth by saying,

> *The Spirit of the Lord is upon Me,*
> *Because He has anointed Me*

To preach the gospel to the poor;
He has sent Me to heal the brokenhearted,
To proclaim liberty to the captives
And recovery of sight to the blind,
To set at liberty those who are oppressed;
To proclaim the acceptable year of the Lord.
Luke 4:18–19

Jesus leaves no doubt and no misunderstanding: His anointing by the Spirit of God is for the purpose of preaching the Gospel to the poor, healing the brokenhearted, setting captives free, and giving sight to the blind. The "Jesus cause" is unparalleled in its scope and unsurpassed in its magnitude—He has come to set the captives free!

The Jesus cause is solely about setting people free from sin, bondage, addictions, shame, and yes, even Hell. Jesus is ready to take on anyone (Pharisees and scribes especially), anything (Jewish rituals, Satan and demons), at any time. His cause is clear and His calling to His disciples is succinct and simple: Follow Me and I will set your heart free. Jesus came to set us free from the mundane, boring, and trivial. Jesus actually looks more like a special ops commando than a surfer boy!

Years ago, while I was working for a leading pastor in California, running his Bible Institute, he made a point one day about discipleship. He said, "Steve, the point of building men is to train them to love Christ, the Church, and His cause." Though there is more to it than just that, this pastor summed up the way of Jesus and the subsequent calling upon His twelve men and all of us.

The cause of Christ, the mission of Christ, is freedom. Freedom in our hearts; freedom to worship; freedom to walk in intimacy with Christ; freedom to set other captives free. This is the greatest cause ever given to humankind. The greatest mission, the most dangerous mission for the twenty-first-century man, is the same one given over two thousand years ago—to set captives free in the power of the Holy Spirit. We begin with our own hearts, but we don't end there. We are set free to set others free.

The Apostle Paul was consumed with the cause of Christ, even if it meant persecution and imprisonment. We observe in the Book of Philippians a man on a mission who has continually paid the price for the cause of Christ, now in shackles for preaching the Gospel. He recognizes that some other men have used it for selfish gain, with ulterior motives— yet this wholehearted disciple still rejoices that the cause of Christ continues to be preached while he is imprisoned,

> *Some indeed preach Christ even from envy and strife, and some also from goodwill: The former preach Christ from selfish ambition, not sincerely, supposing to add affliction to my chains... What then? Only that in every way, whether in pretense or in truth, Christ is preached; and in this I rejoice, yes, and will rejoice.*
> **Philippians 1:15–18**

What an amazing, supernatural attitude! Paul desires that the cause of Christ go forth even if others use it to hurt him, even if their motives aren't pure, and even if it causes him to be imprisoned. Paul is consumed with the Jesus cause.

David's heart was conditioned through worship, prayer, and intimacy with God. His life was set up for the cause of God because the ears of his heart were attuned to the voice of God. David's heart was God's heart, and He could feel the Lord's heartbeat. David was living for God's glory. He was focused on God's majesty being displayed on the earth.

Thus, upon entering a Goliath-saturated valley, David's heart could only cry out, "Is there not a cause?"

What about you? What is the condition of your relationship with Christ? Has God called you to a cause worth living for? Worth dying for? Our next chapter will take a deeper look into the Valley of Elah. Get ready for battle.

The Dangerous Adventure: Day 5

1. What is your Valley of Elah? What are the Goliath-dominated situations in your life?

2. How does our heart relationship with Christ impact our view of the cause of Christ?

3. Are you living your life for the cause of Christ? Why or why not?

4. Are the things you're living for worth dying for?

DAY 6: WARRIOR

1 Samuel 17

31 Now when the words which David spoke were heard, they reported them to Saul; and he sent for him. 32 Then David said to Saul, "Let no man's heart fail because of him; your servant will go and fight with this Philistine."

33 And Saul said to David, "You are not able to go against this Philistine to fight with him; for you are a youth, and he a man of war from his youth."

34 But David said to Saul, "Your servant used to keep his father's sheep, and when a lion or a bear came and took a lamb out of the flock, 35 I went out after it and struck it, and delivered the lamb from its mouth; and when it arose against me, I caught it by its beard, and struck and killed it. 36 Your servant has killed both lion and bear; and this uncircumcised Philistine will be like one of them, seeing he has defied the armies of the living God." 37 Moreover David said, "The Lord, who delivered me from the paw of the lion and from the paw of the bear, He will deliver me from the hand of this Philistine."

And Saul said to David, "Go, and the Lord be with you!"

38 So Saul clothed David with his armor, and he put a bronze helmet on his head; he also clothed him with a coat of mail. 39 David fastened his sword to his armor and tried to walk, for he had not tested them. And David said to Saul, "I cannot walk with these, for I have not tested them." So David took them off.

40 Then he took his staff in his hand; and he chose for himself five smooth stones from the brook, and put them in a shepherd's bag, in a pouch which he had, and his sling was in his hand. And he drew near to the Philistine. 41 So the Philistine came, and began drawing near to David, and the man who bore the shield went before him. 42 And when the Philistine looked about and saw David, he disdained him; for he was only a youth, ruddy and good-looking. 43 So the Philistine said to David, "Am I a dog, that you come to me with sticks?" And the Philistine cursed David by his gods. 44 And the Philistine said to David, "Come to me, and I will give your flesh to the birds of the air and the beasts of the field!"

45 Then David said to the Philistine, "You come to me with a sword, with a spear, and with a javelin. But I come to you in the name of the Lord of hosts, the God of the armies of Israel, whom you have defied. 46 This day the Lord will deliver you into my hand, and I will strike you and take your head from you. And this day I will give the carcasses of the camp of the Philistines to the birds of the air and the wild beasts of the earth, that all the earth may know that there is a God in Israel. 47 Then all this assembly shall know that the Lord does not save with sword and spear; for the battle is the Lord's, and He will give you into our hands."

48 So it was, when the Philistine arose and came and drew near to meet David, that David hurried and ran toward the army to meet the Philistine. 49 Then David put his hand in his bag and took out a stone; and he slung it and struck the Philistine in his forehead, so that the stone sank into his forehead, and he fell on his face to the earth. 50 So David prevailed over the Philistine with a sling and a stone, and struck the Philistine and killed him. But there was no sword in the hand of David. 51 Therefore David ran and stood over the Philistine, took his sword and drew it out of its sheath and killed him, and cut off his head with it. And when the Philistines saw that their champion was dead, they fled.

52 Now the men of Israel and Judah arose and shouted, and pursued the Philistines as far as the entrance of the valley and to the gates of Ekron. And the wounded of the Philistines fell along the road to Shaaraim, even as far as Gath and Ekron. 53 Then the children of Israel returned from chasing the Philistines, and they plundered their tents. 54 And David took the head of the Philistine and brought it to Jerusalem, but he put his armor in his tent.

We entered the Shephelah, a mountainous area in Palestine that follows the Mediterranean plain from the sea to this strategic valley. I was the Bible teacher for a trip to Israel and on this day the bus stopped in the Valley of Elah. We had come to Israel on an historic day—the anniversary of the founding of the modern nation of Israel, May 14th. Fifty years before, on this date in 1948, this valley had become important once again as Israel fought and won her independence against all the Arab nations arrayed against her.

Many warriors have fought in this much-storied valley. The Valley of Elah is where the Muslim chieftain Saladin fought against the knights of the Crusades in the twelfth century. This valley played a key role in the Maccabean wars with Syria a thousand years before.[50] It was also the valley where the fledgling armies of Saul squared off with the most vicious of all intruders, the Philistines.

There is much debate concerning the origins of the Philistines. Some believe they were originally from Crete. Others say Egypt. Several anthropologists say both Crete *and* Egypt. They were known as "the people of the sea," because of their base of operations in biblical times, the modern area known as the Gaza Strip in southwestern Israel, along the Mediterranean. The Philistines were worshippers of gods and goddesses including Dagon, Ashtaroth, and Beelzebub.

When Saul meets the Philistines they are moving east, from the sea, into the mountainous region of southern Israel. Their goal is to capture the high ground near Bethlehem and split Saul's kingdom in two. The Philistines set up their camp on the southern ridge looking over the valley and Israel on the opposite ridge.

> *And a champion went out from the camp of the Philistines, named Goliath, from Gath, whose height was six cubits and a span. He had a bronze helmet on his head, and he was armed with a coat of mail, and the weight of the coat was five thousand shekels of bronze.*
> *1 Samuel 17:4-5*

The situation is ominous for sure. The Philistines controlled the use of iron, which gave them a decided advantage militarily and economically over Israel. Five thousand shekels of bronze are approximately 125 pounds. Goliath was six cubits and a span in height; a cubit was eighteen inches and a span was nine inches, making Goliath about nine feet tall. If this seems like the exaggeration of a biblical writer, think again. Archeology has found houses along the Gaza Strip with beds over eleven feet long—which indicates that there were giants, "men of renown," of the lineage of the Anakin spoken of in Numbers 13. Goliath probably wasn't a Philistine but a mercenary from that region. Impressive, expressive, seemingly invincible! It's no wonder no one wanted to fight.

The Battle for the Heart

Saul and his men failed to grasp that they had entered a battle that was not to be determined by armor and weaponry. Saul's vantage point was ground-level strategy built on the rules of warfare—the rules of man-made tactics. David's perspective was not who had the weapons, who had the iron, or who had the high ground—he envisioned a battle for the high ground of the heart. It had less to do with land than lordship. David said to Saul, "Let no man's *heart* fail because of him [Goliath]; your servant will go and fight with this Philistine." (Italics mine.)[51] David was first a warrior of the heart before he was a warrior in the field.

The battle of the heart is the engagement that determines the destiny of all men. David intuitively understood the deepest clash among the men of Israel was for their hearts. He sensed that the heart of Saul's army was weak and fearful. This is the clarion cry of this young shepherd: "Let no man's heart fail!"

The heart is a man's most vulnerable, most sensitive place. Thus, the attack upon David's own warrior spirit will be his heart. Satan first attacks David's heart through his brother Eliab, who says, "I know your pride and the insolence of your heart."[52] David is a warrior for the heart, and his heart is put on trial by his brother.

There is an older brother in all our lives, vying for supremacy of our heart. The warrior spirit must first be tested in the private conversations, the challenges, the assaults upon our heart. Recently my son who plays college baseball was on a hitting spree, batting over .400 in a six-game stretch, when one of the upper classmen on the team told him he was being selfish in his enthusiasm for the game. What? Being enthusiastic is selfish? It was an attack upon Isaac's heart; the discouragement it caused him led to two errors and a hitting slump. We had to talk through what had happened and recognize it for what it was—an attack upon his heart.

Recently I went through the most difficult struggle of my life: I was attacked as a leader and maligned by men I thought I could trust. The trial was not only the circumstances. It also concerned how I would respond in my heart. I felt devastated and defeated at times. The enemy was attacking my life and calling through assaults on my heart. More on this in a later chapter.

If demons take out a man's heart, they take out his will to fight. Without the will to fight, men crumble. Satan is identified as "the accuser of the brethren, who accuses day and night" (Revelation 12:10). His self-assigned job description is to take out our hearts. This is why Solomon said, "Guard your heart more than anything else, because the source of your life flows from it."[53] David's warrior heart is assaulted through his elder brother, and our hearts will also be assaulted by people, sometimes those closest to us.

The accusations of Satan take the form of assaults upon our heart because that's where we discover our identity. Our identity as God's children, the redeemed, is always at the heart level. Our sexuality, gender, manhood, and struggle to forge who we are and what makes us men lies at the core of Satan's attacks. Why is it that sexual abuse has so much power in creating shame in our hearts? Why is it that the physical beatings and emotional tirades from our fathers still linger in our memories?

David is a warrior for the heart—first his own, but then for the cause of Israel. This is what makes this young man so unique, someone we can learn from. He is a man after God's own heart and—don't miss this— God's own heart is the freedom of your heart! Your heart is free, but you will have to fight for that freedom.

In the movie *Braveheart,* William Wallace's father, Malcolm, has been killed in battle. William has a dream in which Malcolm looks at him and says, "Your heart is free, have the courage to follow it." The rest of William's life is framed against the backdrop of this blessing from his father. Paul said it well: "Stand fast therefore in the liberty by which Christ has made us free, and do not be entangled again with a yoke of bondage."[54]

The warrior fights for his heart because it is from the heart that we discover our identity as men! It all begins and ends at the heart level. We will have to battle through the shameless assaults of the enemy to find our "shame less" warrior heart. Jesus, with a heart set free, for the joy set before Him, "despising the shame," went to the cross!

Assignments From God

David has been given an assignment from God. His heart comes alive with the courageous vision of fighting Goliath, "Your servant will go and fight with this Philistine."[55] David knows exactly what to do, with little hesitation and a confidence from God that is startling. No one else has the faith to fight—only him.

Men, you were made for war. You have been wired by God for spiritual conflict. You were made for assignments from God unique to your gifting and calling. Those assignments result in battles against the enemy that will only be won through warrior hearts. All men have a war to fight, and it's in spiritual war that men are formed. Ruskin wrote in *Crown of Wild Olive*,

> When I tell you that war is the foundation of all the arts, I mean also that it is the foundation of all high virtues and faculties of man. It is very strange to me to discover this, and dreadful, but I saw it to be a most undeniable fact ... I found, in brief, that all great nations learned their truth of word and strength of thought, in war; that they were nourished in war and wasted by peace; taught by war and deceived by peace; trained by war and betrayed by peace; in a word, that they were born in war and expired in peace. .[56]

What a powerful statement. Ruskin leaves us with an interesting thought, "taught by war and deceived by peace; trained by war and betrayed by peace." We will see later, in our journey with David, that this will sadly be true in his life. But it's true for every man. You and I were made for war, for battle, for a cause worth dying for.

Men, "nourished" in war? Now that would unsettle any anchor of our major TV networks. Talk about being politically incorrect! This flies right in the face of everything we hear today about manhood. The soft, kind, metro male might struggle in such an environment. For sure, this even slaps the face of the churchy man we have grown up to act like. We live in a day where the church seemingly has no battles for men to fight! One author recently posted,

> We've exchanged that great hymn "Onward, Christian Soldiers" for a subtle but telling substitute, a song that is currently being taught to thousands of children in Sunday school each week, I may never march in the infantry, ride in the cavalry, shoot the artillery, I may never fly over the enemy but I'm in the Lord's army, yes sir! There is no battle and there is no war and there is no enemy and your life is not at stake and you are not desperately needed this very hour, but you're in the Lord's army. Yes, sir. Doing what? may I ask? .[57]

Each of us has been given assignments from God that will require a warrior heart. Some assignments are constant to our life: If married, you have the constant assignment of fighting for your wife's heart. If you have children, you have the constant assignment of battling for the hearts of your children. My greatest battles as a warrior have been as a husband and father. Liz and I have been married more than thirty years, and through our rocky times we have developed a battle routine of beginning each week, Monday, in fasting and prayer for our marriage and family. With seven children and all the responses we must have for their lives, we have found that without much prayer and significant communication, we just can't make it. The spiritual battles we have fought for our kids have been extreme, and at times, very difficult. We desperately need these times for prayer and preparation.

Once, when one of our sons was going through a significant battle in his life, Liz would stay up all night warring in prayer for him. She and I picked up our fasting routine to more than just one day a week. Because our son was having nightmares and demonic visitations at night, we came into his room and prayed constantly with him. Some nights he even slept in our room, next to our bed. Eventually the battle was won.

We have also been given assignments that may change over time. These are most often related to our jobs. God is sovereign over your life and your job is an assignment from God. You are sent into your work to be a warrior for the cause of Christ. I have known the assignment of God as a missionary to college students in the U.S. and Japan. Now as a pastor/teacher in Colorado, my assignment is built on shepherding the people of the new church I've planted, The Road@Chapel Hills, writing, and speaking in various ministries around the world.

Whose Battle?

We all know the rest of the story. David enters the Valley of Elah with a sling and five smooth stones. The proud, arrogant giant is insulted by Saul's decision to send the little shepherd, and a verbal exchange ensues. Belittled by Goliath, David's response further supports our insight into his heart: "Then all this assembly shall know that the LORD does not save with sword and spear; for the battle *is* the LORD's, and He will give you into our hands." [58] David has no personal vendetta with Goliath. David has not prepared for battle through sharpening his stones or whetting his sling. David knows this battle has been set up, prepared, and orchestrated by God. Though physical in context, it's spiritual in nature. If God has set up the battle, God will fight the battle. David realizes that he is simply a servant of God's sovereignly orchestrated plans. David would later pen this battle hymn:

> *God is my strength and power,*
> *And He makes my way perfect.*
> *He makes my feet like the feet of deer,*
> *And sets me on my high places.*
> *He teaches my hands to make war,*
> *So that my arms can bend a bow of bronze.*
> ***2 Samuel 22:33-35***

There is a certain peace and confidence that we can have when we realize we are following God into His battles. He is living within us and empowering us. Have you ever thought of Jesus as a warrior? If not, take some time to read Revelation 19. "In righteousness He judges and makes war. His eyes were like a flame of fire … Out of His mouth goes a sharp sword" (verses 11-12, 15). You have been recreated in the image of Christ, in His likeness, and you have His very nature pumping through your spiritual veins. You have a war to fight! *The Message* captures this theme.

> This is no afternoon athletic contest that we'll walk away from and forget about in a couple of hours. This is for keeps, a life-or-death fight to the finish against the Devil and all his angels.[59]

God has assignments for battle that are unique to each of us. As men, we are wired to take on spiritual enemies. We need to be trained in how to fight, when to fight, and the fight that truly is "the Lord's." For many, the way they fight is entirely fleshly and carnal. This is not a battle fought through anger, frustration, and pride, but rather a fight for the cause of Christ on the earth as we war for our hearts and the hearts of those around us. David fought with a fierce love of God flowing through intentionality for the glory of God.

It was this kind of warrior heart that propelled Dietrich Bonhoeffer to leave the safety of his job as an American seminary professor and enter the spiritual battle for his country during the rise of Adolf Hitler and the Nazis in his native Germany. As he watched the church in Germany continually acquiesce to the Nazi Party's demands, he was asked to speak at the Fano Conference in Denmark. The context of his message was the fear to oppose Hitler within the Lutheran Church. Bonhoeffer gives new definition to our understanding of "safety" as it relates to the battles of God,

> There is no way to peace along the way of safety. For peace must be dared, it is itself the great venture and can never be safe. Peace is the opposite of security. To demand 'guarantees' is to want to protect oneself. Peace means giving oneself completely to God's commandment, wanting no security, but in faith and obedience laying the destiny of the nations in the hand of Almighty God, not trying to direct it for selfish purposes. Battles are won, not with weapons, but with God. They are won when the way leads to the cross.[60]

David is not considering his own safety or the preservation of his life as he takes on Goliath. He knows the battle is the Lord's. He knows that where God guides, God provides. He is the One who has called him into a battle to fight, and He is the One who will do the fighting through him.

Men, you have been given an assignment from God for a war to fight. It is a unique Valley of Elah set up by God for you. No one can fight your battles. In a real sense, you cannot even fight your own battles—God will fight the battle through you. He wants to use your warrior heart to fight His battles. He is calling you into the war that you are distinctively wired to fight.

So, the question you might have is, how do we fight? How do we enter God's Valleys of Elah to fight His battles? In our next chapter, we will look at how God uniquely prepared David, and will prepare you, for a lifetime of spiritual warfare.

The Dangerous Adventure: Day 6

1. What are the assignments God has given you to fight?

2. How's it going for you?

3. What are your deepest fears in this battle?

DAY 7: LIONS

1 Samuel 17

33 And Saul said to David, "You are not able to go against this Philistine to fight with him; for you are a youth, and he a man of war from his youth."

34 But David said to Saul, "Your servant used to keep his father's sheep, and when a lion or a bear came and took a lamb out of the flock, 35 I went out after it and struck it, and delivered the lamb from its mouth; and when it arose against me, I caught it by its beard, and struck and killed it. 36 Your servant has killed both lion and bear; and this uncircumcised Philistine will be like one of them, seeing he has defied the armies of the living God." 37 Moreover David said, "The Lord, who delivered me from the paw of the lion and from the paw of the bear, He will deliver me from the hand of this Philistine."

And Saul said to David, "Go, and the Lord be with you!"

David defeated Goliath in the Valley of Elah because he had defeated lions and bears beforehand. God uniquely prepared him for Elah through the tests in Bethlehem. David may have looked like some Johnny-come-lately to Saul, but God had known David intimately for years. David had been tested, prepared, and was now ready for the biggest confrontation of his young life.

Upon being rebuked by Saul that he was only a boy and, unlike the mercenary Goliath, not a "man of war," David's response is telling of what God has been doing in the secret places of his heart. In the secret is the secret!

Battling bears and lions? Are you kidding me? Real bears! Real lions!

WORSHIPPER WARRIOR

David has wrestled lambs away from the mouths of lions and bears and then killed them.

Lions are some of the deadliest animals in the world. They are considered the fourth most dangerous to humans in sub-Saharan Africa, just behind the black mamba snake and Nile crocodile (which is the only predator to the lion). Many experts believe they might be the most ferocious of all if they were not limited to animal preserves. One world-renowned hunter who is known for his guided hunts with lions has said that "without a doubt, the lion is the most dangerous animal" he has ever hunted.

A 2005 study showed that lion attacks on man were on the rise in Tanzania and Mozambique due to the encroachment into their natural habitats. Every year, thousands of humans are mauled and killed by lions in spite of being limited to protected areas. A lion can run at speeds up to fifty miles (about eighty-one kilometers) per hour. A male lion's body is about six or seven feet (about two meters) long. That's not including the tail, which is about three feet (one meter) long. The male lion can weigh up to 550 pounds and is known to attack and kill elephants!

What about bears? I live in Colorado, where black bears are growing in numbers across the Rocky Mountains. Once while hunting elk, I crested a mountain and came face-to-face with a mother bear and her three cubs next to a bloody deer carcass. The bear noticed my movements and stood up to her full six feet. My pulse was pounding as I slowly raised my rifle. I slid behind a tree, and the bear moved away. But just a few minutes in the presence of such power, wildness, and brawny strength made my knees quake. After she left, I sat down for a moment just to collect my scattered wits and wipe my perspiring neck.

David's field of experience is no Country Bear Jamboree life, but real warfare. David comes to the public arena of war because his God-confidence has been built in the private victories waged with only One in the audience. Private battles are the testing ground for public battles still to wage. Private battles are waged with only two in attendance—oneself and God.

The lions of David's life created his warrior heart. David had learned on the hills of Bethlehem, as a shepherd, that if he didn't act, if he didn't fight back, he would see his lambs, one by one, picked off by his carnivorous enemies. David learned to act because there was no one else to depend on. It was him and his sheep. He was responsible for the sheep—they were his assignment from God. His options were to cut and run or to stand and fight.

I have often wondered how David dealt with fear. Fear is the greatest enemy of the most challenging situations. For some, fear incapacitates and paralyzes. For others, fear drives them forward. Facing and processing fear may be the greatest test of God's training in David's life. Fear is conquered only by being tested in fearful situations. David had been tested in a spiritual boot camp of God's choosing.

Boot Camp

I have close friend, a retired Army lieutenant colonel. In talking about Army boot camp, he said, "Arriving at Fort Benning, Georgia, Basic training was all about fear. We literally could not pee without permission. It is eight weeks of hell, designed to teach eighteen-, nineteen-, and twenty-year-old kids to march, run in formation, and fire a weapon. It begins with fear. We are afraid of everything! Most of the boys in my training cycle, upon arrival, didn't know how to do anything, much less fight. But by the end of boot camp we were confident and ready for almost any situation. Graduating from basic training was no longer about fear. It was the understanding that this was the beginning of a journey toward becoming soldiers to which we had to soberly focus our hearts and minds."

The purpose of Army boot camp is training for battle through conquering fear. I believe that is true in all our lives. God tests us in His unique boot camps in order to take us into fear and intimidation. It is only as we conquer our fears through faith that we become ready for the battles the Lord has for us to fight.

David has learned to conquer his fears. In his most famous poem, Psalm 23, he writes, "Yea, though I walk through the valley of the shadow of death, I will fear no evil, for You are with me." David has learned to battle with and fight through his fears. He has learned that the presence and power of God are with him in every valley and challenge he faces. In the boot camps of God, he mastered fear.

Throughout the Psalms, David speaks of his training ground, but in Psalm 144 he elaborates on what God did to train him and how God fought for him in battles against fierce foes. David writes,

> *Blessed be the Lord my Rock, Who trains my hands for war,*
> *And my fingers for battle—*
> *My lovingkindness and my fortress,*
> *My high tower and my deliverer,*
> *My shield and the One in whom I take refuge,*
> *Who subdues my people under me ...*
> *Stretch out Your hand from above;*
> *Rescue me and deliver me out of great waters,*
> *From the hand of foreigners ...*
> **Psalm 144:1-7**

David recognizes that God has been His trainer, His mentor, His commander. He has learned to recognize that God Himself has trained his abilities, his gifting, and his leadership. God is the One who has led him and equipped him. For David to say to the mercenary giant from Gath, "the battle is the Lord's" is a learned response, learned through hardship and seasoned through battle.

What is most interesting about this Psalm is that David has been given insight into the purpose of his spiritual boot camp, the training of God— battle! David understands that life is a battle. For him, it was constant and daily. As you read further in this book, one thing that will stand out is the constant faith and resilience David has to pull up because of the many battles he will have to fight.

As the years go by, David will learn there will be lions to fight in many arenas of his life. He will learn to conquer fear through sheer courage learned in battle. He will have to fight foes on every front—from physical battlefields of hand-to-hand conflict to the emotional battlefields of relationships and love. Pat Benatar captures the heart of David and the battle for love in her haunting song, "Love Is a Battlefield."

Love is a battlefield. Marriage is a battlefield. Our job is a battlefield. Guess what? Life is a battlefield! Most of us are not equipped for this battle of life. Most of us men feel way out of our comfort zone in the relationships we find ourselves engaged in. I know Liz and I came into marriage ill-prepared for the war zone of living with each other. Liz came out of a divorced family—and though my family of origin was intact, I was twenty-seven years old, already a missionary, and fiercely independent. It was a fuse ready to be lit on the stick of dynamite called relational conflict.

This is not a book on marriage (though I have written one, The God-Wild Marriage, published in 2012) and I will not elaborate on this topic. Suffice to say that if you are married or plan to be in the future, your most fierce spiritual and emotional battles will be fought on the fronts of marriage and parenting. It will be in the kitchen and bedroom of your life that God will introduce you to the most important boot camp of warfare.

God has wired each man for battle, and His will is to equip you for the unique battles of your life. He has you in His boot camp to train you for spiritual warfare that can only be won when you fight those battles His way with His weapons.

As a father, husband, and pastor, I am convinced that the purpose of the home and the purpose of the church are one and the same: They are equipping centers for building wholehearted Jesus followers who can win in the battles of life. My purpose as a husband and father is to train and build wholehearted, fully devoted, Spirit-empowered, Word-grounded disciples of Jesus. My purpose as a pastor is to build a church full of wholehearted, fully committed, Word-saturated, Spirit-led Jesus disciples.

It's that simple and it's that complex.

Every Man's Lion

A large part of my life as a missionary and pastor has been the ministry of working with, discipling, and counseling men. Whether they are missionaries, pastors, or the working men of my churches, every man's battlefield looks the same. Every man has lions, those battlefield situations that are not unique but average for being of the male gender in a world controlled and manipulated by Satan. In Ephesians, Paul speaks of Satan's power over our world as "the course of this world, [controlled] according to the prince of the power of the air."[61] Paul calls it a course, a challenge given to us as people of God that works against us, defies us, and constantly attempts to control us.

I have come to believe there are three great lions that each man must face and conquer if he is to be mightily used by God. In my own life, these areas have been my undoing and my struggles. We all can see the wiles of the devil unleashed over our lives in these key areas. We could write a book on each one, and some authors have done so, but suffice to say that awareness is the beginning of power.

The three lions of every man's life are sexual passion; self-reliance; and shame. Each will be covered later in this book in more detail. David struggled with each, and it was his defeats and eventual victories that make his life so instructive for our own.

The lion of sexual passion gives us the opportunity to discover our God-ordained identity. The lion of self-reliance and pride helps us discover our true dependence. The lion of shame shows us the power of vulnerability and our need for brothers. I will share more on all of this in the later chapters.

Every Man's Sling

It is instructive that Paul, in writing to young men who had just come out of paganism, self-made men who had known the world of temple prostitution and sexual ecstasies (the Temple of Artemis was known all over the world for its sexual practices), spoke of the proper boundaries and joy of a God-filled life of battle. In Chapter Five of the letter to the Ephesians, Paul gives the most definitive description in all of Scripture of how to conduct oneself in marriage, in work, and in relationships with the opposite sex. It is in that context that Paul introduces God's battle plan:

> *Finally, my brethren, be strong in the Lord and in the power of His might. Put on the whole armor of God, that you may be able to stand against the wiles of the devil. For we do not wrestle against flesh and blood, but against principalities, against powers, against the rulers of the darkness of this age, against spiritual hosts of wickedness in the heavenly places.*
> **Ephesians 6:10-12**

Paul wanted the Ephesians to clearly understand that the life of work and family was a battleground. He wanted them to grasp the power to be wholehearted Jesus disciples through a battle plan that involved God's armor. Paul was no hand-holding, weak-kneed, sappy, philosophical counselor. He was more like a seasoned colonel leading his troops into battle. Paul is essentially saying that life is a battle, and you better be ready to fight with God's armor in the power of His might.

Paul is writing more like a Maximus in the movie *Gladiator*, encouraging his bloody, worn-down Roman troops against the Germanic hordes of the north, "Hold the line, stay with me! What we do in life echoes in eternity!" This is the spirit of Paul. This is the world we live in. Like Paul, we are engaged in a battle that can only be fought and won through the power of the Holy Spirit and with the weapons of God.

He was saying this is a pitched, decisive fight to the death that can't be won without a warrior heart. We all must face this reality in life. The sling of the Davidic warrior is then spelled out clearly and concisely:

> *Therefore take up the whole armor of God, that you may be able to withstand in the evil day, and having done all, to stand. Stand therefore, having girded your waist with truth, having put on the breastplate of righteousness, and having shod your feet with the preparation of the gospel of peace; above all, taking the shield of*

faith with which you will be able to quench all the fiery darts of the wicked one. And take the helmet of salvation, and the sword of the Spirit, which is the word of God; praying always with all prayer and supplication in the Spirit, being watchful to this end with all perseverance and supplication for all the saints
Ephesians 6:13-18

Paul not only spells out the battle, he gives us the strategy for victory. The struggles for purity and the warfare to keep a marriage together are part of the true sling of victory. In the defeats, failures, and shame of my life, I have had to discover and rediscover the truth of the above passage. It has been my daily experience that only when we learn to proactively put on the armor of God can we develop a warrior heart.

It is only as we put on the armor, figuratively and actively praying on the pieces, that we find victory in our unique battles. I am discovering that only when I begin each day with what I call The Warrior Prayer am I able to consistently win against the temptations and strategies of the devil. Try it out. See what God will do when you follow the guidance of The Warrior Prayer each day. Start today. Put on the armor and watch God become your warrior in your unique fight,

Lord Jesus, I acknowledge today that I cannot withstand the temptations that come my way without Your power and strength. I cannot handle the lions that come my way without Your guidance, wisdom, and insight. Empower me to have a warrior heart. Today, I am going to put on Your full armor and withstand all the power of Satan and his demons. I now put on the helmet of salvation. I thank You for saving me, healing me, and releasing me from the domain of darkness. I praise You that I am a new creation in Christ and that the old is passed away. Renew my mind with the truth that I can do all things through Christ who strengthens me. I put on the breastplate of righteousness, which protects my heart. I thank You that I have a new heart, a loving heart, a soft heart. Lord, guide me in my motives and purposes in relationships. Watch over my heart to love You with all my heart and to love my neighbors with the same heart that I love myself. I put on the belt of truth and ask You to speak to me from Your Word, the Bible. Empower me to believe truth and stand on truth today. Jesus, I pick up the shield of faith and ask You to enlarge my faith. Use my faith to extinguish the temptations and strategies of the enemy. Increase my faith to trust You and believe in You even when struggles come my way. Holy Spirit, I pick up the sword of the

Spirit, the Word of God, and read it today. I will love Your Word and obey what You are saying to me. I will let the Scriptures be the first and last word to me on matters of faith and practice. Lastly, Father, I shod my feet with the gospel of peace. May I be a peacemaker in all my relationships. Guide me into situations where I can model and present the Prince of Peace to this world. I now stand in Your armor for this day. Fill me with Your Holy Spirit. Amen.

The Dangerous Excursion: Day 7

1. How do you personally relate to concept that, "Love is a Battlefield?"

2. What kind of a spiritual boot camp have you been experiencing through the tests of God?

3. What are the lions in your life right now? How are you managing these battles?

4. Set a time each morning to pray The Warrior Prayer.

DAY 8: ENEMIES

1 Samuel 18

5 So David went out wherever Saul sent him, and behaved wisely. And Saul set him over the men of war, and he was accepted in the sight of all the people and also in the sight of Saul's servants. 6 Now it had happened as they were coming home, when David was returning from the slaughter of the Philistines, that the women had come out of all the cities of Israel, singing and dancing, to meet King Saul, with tambourines, with joy, and with musical instruments. 7 So the women sang as they danced, and said:

"Saul has slain his thousands And David his ten thousands."

8 Then Saul was very angry, and the saying displeased him; and he said, "They have ascribed to David ten thousands, and to me they have ascribed only thousands. Now what more can he have but the kingdom?" 9 So Saul eyed David from that day forward.

10 And it happened on the next day that the distressing spirit from God came upon Saul, and he prophesied inside the house. So David played music with his hand, as at other times; but there was a spear in Saul's hand. 11 And Saul cast the spear, for he said, "I will pin David to the wall!" But David escaped his presence twice.

12 Now Saul was afraid of David, because the Lord was with him, but had departed from Saul. 13 Therefore Saul removed him from his presence, and made him his captain over a thousand; and he went out and came in before the people. 14 And David behaved wisely in all his ways, and the Lord was with him. 15 Therefore, when Saul saw that he behaved very wisely, he was afraid of him. 16 But all Israel and Judah loved David, because he went out and came in before them.

17 Then Saul said to David, "Here is my older daughter Merab; I will give her to you as a wife. Only be valiant for me, and fight the Lord's battles." For Saul thought, "Let my hand not be against him, but let the hand of the Philistines be against him."

18 So David said to Saul, "Who am I, and what is my life or my father's family in Israel, that I should be son-in-law to the king?" 19 But it happened at the time when Merab, Saul's daughter, should have been given to David, that she was given to Adriel the Meholathite as a wife.

20 *Now Michal, Saul's daughter, loved David. And they told Saul, and the thing pleased him. 21 So Saul said, "I will give her to him, that she may be a snare to him, and that the hand of the Philistines may be against him." Therefore Saul said to David a second time, "You shall be my son-in-law today."*

22 *And Saul commanded his servants, "Communicate with David secretly, and say, 'Look, the king has delight in you, and all his servants love you. Now therefore, become the king's son-in-law.'"*

23 *So Saul's servants spoke those words in the hearing of David. And David said, "Does it seem to you a light thing to be a king's son-in-law, seeing I am a poor and lightly esteemed man?" 24 And the servants of Saul told him, saying, "In this manner David spoke."*

25 *Then Saul said, "Thus you shall say to David: 'The king does not desire any dowry but one hundred foreskins of the Philistines, to take vengeance on the king's enemies.'" But Saul thought to make David fall by the hand of the Philistines. 26 So when his servants told David these words, it pleased David well to become the king's son-in-law. Now the days had not expired; 27 therefore David arose and went, he and his men, and killed two hundred men of the Philistines. And David brought their foreskins, and they gave them in full count to the king, that he might become the king's son-in-law. Then Saul gave him Michal his daughter as a wife.*

28 *Thus Saul saw and knew that the Lord was with David, and that Michal, Saul's daughter, loved him; 29 and Saul was still more afraid of David. So Saul became David's enemy continually. 30 Then the princes of the Philistines went out to war. And so it was, whenever they went out, that David behaved more wisely than all the servants of Saul, so that his name became highly esteemed.*

All of us are surprised at some point in our lives that everyone doesn't like us just the way we are. For some, this happens with the shock of the kindergarten world; for others, through your siblings or kids in the neighborhood. Sooner or later, there is a time when we all have to leave the nurture of mom and the security of our home and enter the environment of enmity and jealousy.

David's time for that has come. Even after doing all he's been asked—from worship to warfare—he begins to feel the pressure of animosity from his king. David's life will be impacted deeply from these days onward. The reality of enemies and enmity will form much of David's spirituality.

We find the words "enemy" and "enemies" mentioned 104 times in the Book of Psalms. Most people never think of the Psalms in relation to persecution from enemies, but that will shape much of David's prayer life and worship. This is primarily what makes David the most unique character in the Bible—how he handles enemies, envy, and enmity. David sheds light on this thorny issue more than anyone else.

How we react to enemies will form much of our spiritual lives as well. How we respond to teasing, bullying, being snubbed, excluded, critiqued, stabbed in the back, and betrayed is one of the most challenging arenas of our walk with God as men. The world of competition, compromise, and ambition is the world we men live in through our jobs, our family, and even in the church. It is demanding and often unfair.

Recently, a close friend of mine resigned from a job he had been very successful at due to a changing work environment that would have involved compromising his integrity to reach the bottom line. It was clear that his stand on certain issues was creating animosity among his peers. Friends became enemies virtually overnight.

American Dream Not

For many in America, the Christian life is gift-wrapped as the American Dream. The American Dream Christianity of many churches looks like life just gets better and better, we get richer and richer, and our friends love us more and more. Having enemies and suffering are not part of this teaching. This is why so many fall away and drop off when tough times come. And come they will.

Read the Bible! The lives of the biblical heroes are full of enemies, obstacles, and difficulties. It's part and parcel of following Jesus. It is the way of discipleship. Jesus promised that it would be hard. *"These things I have spoken to you, that in Me you may have peace. In the world you will have tribulation; but be of good cheer, I have overcome the world."*[62] We *will* have tribulation; we *will* experience enemies who oppose us. Prepare for it. If it hasn't come yet, it will. Flaming missiles are coming your way.

This is exactly why we put on the armor in The Warrior Prayer daily.

Gathering Storm

In Psalm 18, Saul is growing increasingly deranged and demonized. David's predicament is puzzling. All he's done has been good and positive for Saul: Saul's psychic darkness leaves him whenever David worships; Saul's most violent enemies, the Philistines, are at bay, due to David's continual bravery. David is good for Saul's kingdom. He keeps doing the right things under tremendous pressure. And that is actually the problem— Saul hates David's goodness.

David's willingness to serve and love his king, fight for the kingdom, and leave his family to be a comfort to Saul is met with increasing violence and jealousy. Instead of healing there is hatred. Instead of friendship there is enmity. Scripture says, "Saul was afraid of David because the Lord was with him," and then, "Saul was yet more afraid of David; and Saul became David's enemy continually." The storm is gathering around David.

Saul tries to murder David the first time during a worship session. David's anointing as a worshipper had first caught Saul's attention, but now it fuels his jealousy. So, Saul hurls his spear at David's head twice and misses. He then plans to give him his daughter in marriage with the condition that he proves his bravery in battle. And just as David agrees and carries out the plan, Saul changes his mind and gives his daughter to another man.

Knowing one of his other daughters, Michal, wants to marry David, Saul agrees with the hope that she will be a snare to him. Saul invents another situation to have David killed, demanding the gruesome task of collecting one hundred foreskins from the Philistines. David goes out and kills two hundred Philistines and gladly gives the foreskins to Saul. This only aggravates the king more.

Saul now enlists the help of a ninja-like assassin team, sending them to David's home (1 Samuel 18). Instead of a snare, Michal becomes an informant when she learns of the plot. She invokes some ancient code of honor that keeps the assassins at bay by saying David is sick in bed. Saul has no such code of honor, and demands that his ninjas just barge in, pick up the bed with David in it, and bring it to him so he can kill David himself. In the meantime, David rappels out his window and escapes.

Be the Person God Can Defend

The title to Psalm 59 reads, "To the Chief Musician. Set to 'Do Not Destroy,' a Michtam of David When Saul Sent Men, and They Watched the House in Order to Kill Him."[63] David, the poet, musician, and songwriter, during this time of intense pressure might have actually prayed this prayer while still in his house, thinking through what to do next. He might have pulled away in the wilderness, while on the run, and shared his deepest feelings with the Lord. Inspired by God, this poem gives us tremendous insight into how to deal with real adversaries who oppose us. David, who as far as we can see from Scripture is purely innocent of wrongdoing, still has enemies who hate him. Under such pressure, he cries out to God from an innocent but betrayed heart,

> *Deliver me from my enemies, O my God;*
> *Defend me from those who rise up against me.*
> *Deliver me from the workers of iniquity,*
> *And save me from bloodthirsty men.*
> *For look, they lie in wait for my life;*
> *The mighty gather against me,*
> *Not for my transgression nor for my sin, O Lord*
> ***Psalm 59:1-3***

First, take note that David calls them "enemies." I'm not speaking of disagreements or misunderstandings with people, but enemies. Enemies are those who actively oppose you, even in some cases, hate you. It may come as a surprise to some of us that some will hate our faith, our calling, our mandate from God. Yes, the stands you take, the convictions you live by, will be opposed. Especially in our unchristian American culture.

As a Jesus disciple who is growing to be a worshipper and warrior, you will have enemies. Sometimes they will be fellow believers! Yes, those who once called you "brother." Paul, in writing to the believers in Phillippi, said, "Don't be terrified by your adversaries" (Philippians 1:28). Jesus told us that brother would betray brother in the latter days. We should not be surprised. Peter, who was familiar with slander and persecution, instructs us to not be surprised by the fiery ordeals we are experiencing (1 Peter 4:12).

David is taking this to the Lord in prayer. David is bold as a lion in his prayer (Proverbs 28:1) against his enemies. He asks God to defend him, deliver him, and cries out to God to do the fighting on his behalf. In Romans 8:31 we read, "If God *is* for us, who *can be* against us?" David knows he's innocent, but he never searches for a public forum to win an argument; rather, he takes his betrayal and wounded heart to the Lord privately. There is no mention anywhere of an open appeal to Saul or his friend Jonathan to get things worked out. David clings to God, crying out only to Him for justice and defense.

We must be a person God can defend. David is. He knows he has had integrity in his work—his enemies have nothing on him. David understands God will defend him against ruthless men, because he is a man whom God can defend. This is a new test for David: the test of enemies opposing the call on his life.

Men, don't be surprised, intimidated, or fearful of attacks against you. Follow David's lead and cling to the Lord during such times; cry out to Him in prayer. Leave it in his hands to defend you. Don't defend yourself! How we respond to accusations will say more about us than about our enemies. There are lessons to be learned in times of enemy attack that cannot be learned any other way.

Free R&D

It is in such times, when enemies rise up, that God is preparing you for a promotion in the Spirit. God's promotions in the Kingdom are gained through experiential knowledge learned in the training center of the wilderness. In times of intense attack, we have the opportunity to access free research and development from our enemies. Rarely are we like David, with literally no malice or sin in our lives. Often it is through our enemies that God shows us our shortcomings, our blind spots that need to be worked on. God can use our enemies to accentuate areas of our life that are not altogether godly or holy.

I recall a time in my life when I was under attack from several directions—all of which deeply wounded my heart. But as I took time away—in daily prayer walks, through personal counseling, and journaling—God slowly began to show me my faults and my pride. It was very difficult to admit how much my reputation and what people thought about me mattered. God was using my friends who had become my enemies to do free R&D on my life.

If we can cultivate a teachable and humble spirit, God can use such times to show us how insecure we really are. Most of us are way more insecure than we think we are. Our insecurities are most often blind spots. Rarely do our friends have the courage to discuss those blind spots with us, so unfortunately, God often uses accusers to shine the light on them. But if we will take these obstacles and turn them into opportunities to learn and grow, we will find ourselves getting stronger in the process.

Often it is our responsibility to go to the person, the accuser, and ask for forgiveness (Matthew 5:22-24). If we have done something wrong, if we have sinned against someone, we should do everything possible to make things right. We are to do everything possible to work things out privately. Not in the public arena of self-defense. In such times, God is showing us our blind spots in order to promote us to a deeper level of maturity.

Promotions in the Spirit

If we choose to receive all that God is saying to us through such battles, He will promote us! God wants to promote you to a new level of spiritual authority and power in your life. Learn from your accusers. God takes us through seasons of attacks and enmity when He is preparing us for promotion, new opportunities to be used by Him. Our response to the attacks will determine the timing and level of promotion.

Don't forget that Satan often knows of God's work in our life before we do. I don't understand it all, but it seems for example that Satan understood that Jesus was about to launch out in his public ministry and so tempted Him toward compromise during his forty days of prayer and fasting (see Matthew 4 and Luke 4). Satan knew of Jesus' plan to go to the cross and spoke through Peter to dissuade Him from His purpose. Jesus told Satan through Peter, "Get behind Me, Satan! You are an offense to Me, for you are not mindful of the things of God, but the things of men."[64] The Enemy (capital *E*, Satan) will usually use enemies (small *e*, people) to get us off track just before God is going to use us in a mighty way!

Attacks from people are often attacks from Satan. He doesn't come at us dressed up with horns and a cape, but rather disguises himself through people. And to make matters worse, most often the Accuser of the Brethren (Revelation 12:10) works through those who call themselves Christians.

Attacks often precede a great work God has for you. They are intended to take us off course, to confuse us, to change the conversation of our heart. The Accuser wants to accuse you before God can promote you! But you must respond in the Spirit, not react in the flesh.

That's the temptation—to dial up the argument and defend ourselves. This is our natural tendency. This is the natural reaction of our old heart. But we have been given a new heart; the heart of stone has been replaced with a heart that is soft and intimate with the Lord. This is the heart of a growing worshipper and warrior. This is God's heart; this is exactly what David possessed and we all long for.

When we become involved in the fight to defend ourselves, we change the conversation of our heart. Instead of seeking the Lord with reverence, joy, and intimacy, we begin to dwell on what others are saying about us. We rehearse the argument in our mind, we start having internal conversations that cause us to overthink the problem, defend ourselves in our heart, and frustrate the plans of God over our lives. When we fight with human ingenuity we are fighting in the flesh. Paul understood this and instructed us,

> *For though we walk in the flesh, we do not war according to the flesh. For the weapons of our warfare are not carnal but mighty in God for pulling down strongholds, casting down arguments and every high thing that exalts itself against the knowledge of God, bringing every thought into captivity to the obedience of Christ.* **2 Corinthians 2:3**

Capture your thoughts, make them POWs of your heart. Turn the arguments against you into prayers of power. Don't defend yourself! Fight in the Spirit through prayer. Let God defend you. If you take your anxiety and fears to the Lord, He will fight for you. If you are standing for what is dear to the Lord, He will defend you. God takes your stand personally. He is using all of this to promote you to a new level of trust in Him. So, trust Him now and recognize there will be rewards later.

God is setting us up for a promotion that only comes as we wage war in the Spirit—privately, not publicly. Don't draw back in fear or intimidation. Don't let your detractors take you off course. Look at each accusation as an opportunity for God to promote you by learning from it and responding in love and prayer. Don't change the conversation of your heart. Fulfill your calling through taking all things to the Lord in prayer and letting Him fight your battles for you.

David then continues with these words, "*Scatter them by your power, and bring them down, O Lord our shield.*"[65] We pay forward when we realize there will be an accounting on God's terms. God is actually preparing you for a promotion if you will respond rightly. If your enemies are opposing the things of God, they are God's enemies too. He will take care of them in His own time. They are not a worry for you. They are not a concern to you. Leave it in God's hands.

David has discovered one of the greatest truths of his life as he now sings of God's deliverance, "To you, O my Strength, I will sing praises; for God is my defense, my God of mercy!"[66] David, this young man who is barely able to shave, is learning the great lesson of God's defense of his life and calling. God has called David to a new promotion in the Spirit. It will be years before he discovers all that God has for him, but David's response to God's interview qualifies him for a work he has been called to do.

So it is with us. God is using enemies to promote us. Don't fight the missiles of the enemy with your own missiles but rather, through The Warrior Prayer, put up the shield of faith and let God extinguish the fiery darts. If you have enemies, rejoice! God is promoting you to a beautiful work He is forming in and through you. Bless those who persecute you by *not* responding in like manner. Much of your spirituality as a worshipper and warrior will be formed through enemies.

The Dangerous Excursion: Day 8

1. Are you experiencing attacks from enemies in your life right now? If so, how are you responding?

2. What can you see as the positive God is teaching you through this ordeal?

3. As you look back over past trials and enemy attacks, how has God used them to promote you, to develop you into a more mature man of God?

DAY 9: ALLIES

1 Samuel 22

1David therefore departed from there and escaped to the cave of Adullam. So when his brothers and all his father's house heard it, they went down there to him. 2 And everyone who was in distress, everyone who was in debt, and everyone who was discontented gathered to him. So he became captain over them. And there were about four hundred men with him.

3 Then David went from there to Mizpah of Moab; and he said to the king of Moab, "Please let my father and mother come here with you, till I know what God will do for me." 4 So he brought them before the king of Moab, and they dwelt with him all the time that David was in the stronghold.

5 Now the prophet Gad said to David, "Do not stay in the stronghold; depart, and go to the land of Judah." So David departed and went into the forest of Hereth.

6 When Saul heard that David and the men who were with him had been discovered—now Saul was staying in Gibeah under a tamarisk tree in Ramah, with his spear in his hand, and all his servants standing about him— 7 then Saul said to his servants who stood about him, "Hear now, you Benjamites! Will the son of Jesse give every one of you fields and vineyards, and make you all captains of thousands and captains of hundreds? 8 All of you have conspired against me, and there is no one who reveals to me that my son has made a covenant with the son of Jesse; and there is not one of you who is sorry for me or reveals to me that my son has stirred up my servant against me, to lie in wait, as it is this day."

9 Then answered Doeg the Edomite, who was set over the servants of Saul, and said, "I saw the son of Jesse going to Nob, to Ahimelech the son of Ahitub. 10 And he inquired of the Lord for him, gave him provisions, and gave him the sword of Goliath the Philistine."

11 So the king sent to call Ahimelech the priest, the son of Ahitub, and all his father's house, the priests who were in Nob. And they all came to the king. 12 And Saul said, "Hear now, son of Ahitub!"

He answered, "Here I am, my lord."

13 Then Saul said to him, "Why have you conspired against me, you and the son of Jesse, in that you have given him bread and a sword, and have inquired of God for him, that he should rise against me, to lie in wait, as it is this day?"

14 So Ahimelech answered the king and said, "And who among all your servants is as faithful as David, who is the king's son-in-law, who goes at your bidding, and is honorable in your house? 15 Did I then begin to inquire of God for him? Far be it from me! Let not the king impute anything to his servant, or to any in the house of my father. For your servant knew nothing of all this, little or much."

16 And the king said, "You shall surely die, Ahimelech, you and all your father's house!" 17 Then the king said to the guards who stood about him, "Turn and kill the priests of the Lord, because their hand also is with David, and because they knew when he fled and did not tell it to me." But the servants of the king would not lift their hands to strike the priests of the Lord. 18 And the king said to Doeg, "You turn and kill the priests!" So Doeg the Edomite turned and struck the priests, and killed on that day eighty-five men who wore a linen ephod. 19 Also Nob, the city of the priests, he struck with the edge of the sword, both men and women, children and nursing infants, oxen and donkeys and sheep—with the edge of the sword.

20 Now one of the sons of Ahimelech the son of Ahitub, named Abiathar, escaped and fled after David. 21 And Abiathar told David that Saul had killed the Lord's priests. 22 So David said to Abiathar, "I knew that day, when Doeg the Edomite was there, that he would surely tell Saul. I have caused the death of all the persons of your father's house. 23 Stay with me; do not fear. For he who seeks my life seeks your life, but with me you shall be safe."

After watching the final movie of *The Lord of the Rings* trilogy, one of my sons asked me, "What was the most meaningful part of the three movies?" We were warming ourselves on a chilly night around our backyard fire pit. We had just enjoyed hot coffee and s'mores, and I was relaxed. It did not take any time at all for me to answer. Where I was most impacted at the heart level through Tolkien's masterful work was not the battles or heroics, but rather "the fellowship of the ring," the friendships of the little band of hobbits.

It was the ferocious love, the continual unending allegiance to a cause, and the devotion to friendship forged in battle. Even at the risk of their own lives, each hobbit never strayed from something greater than friendship—a loyalty that seemed to echo the words of Christ, "Greater love has no one than this, than to lay down one's life for his friends."[67] The modern word I would use is not just "fellowship" (that's too religious for me), nor "friends" (too meaningless today), but rather, "allies."

The word *ally* means, "to enter into an alliance; a person ... that is associated with another or others for some common cause or purpose."[68] That describes what every man desperately needs. It is no mistake that we have since named the fire pit on our property the "Fellowship of the Ring."

Bloodstained

Every man needs allies. Bloodstained allies, because those are the only kind. Allies without blood and battle aren't worth their salt when tough times come. We need the kind of men who have known deep fear and understand the heart issues of life's battles. What men need are heart-level, gut-checked, real battle-trained friends who won't cut and run under pressure. They are bomb-proof, steady. Men need such men.

Most friendships or accountability groups we have in our churches and men's groups are not bloodstained, they are not steady, and most of the time, they never get past the superficial. Allies are not men who just go fly-fishing together and talk about Bible verses while hiding their pornography habits. What I mean are men we can trust, be honest with, and fight heart battles alongside. I use the term "bloodstained" for a reason: They are men who identify honestly with each other's personal battles and drop the religious crap at the door. These are men who will call out our sin, share their own, but then stick with us in times of deep struggle.

In *Gladiator,* as Maximus enters the Roman arena with his band of bloodstained, tested slaves, the circle of upturned shields in the face of attacking chariots saves their lives. Without the impenetrable circle of shields and spears, they are dead men. As they battle the speed of the attacking chariots, Maximus rallies his men to fight together and protect each other through the bravery and tenacity of each man doing his job.

Allies at Adullam

It is fascinating to observe how rapidly allegiances can change. Everyone has abandoned David—even those he had led in battle while fighting Saul's enemies just days before. David, who had been trending as the most popular fighter in Israel, has gone from hero to zero in a week. Saul controlled the social media of the time, and those who loved David now hated him. He was on the IDF Most Wanted list.

The men who had rallied to his side against Goliath, fought shoulder to shoulder against the Philistines, and stood on the streets crying out, "David has killed his ten thousands," are now trying to hunt him down. If there's one thing we can say about human nature, it's how quickly men will turn their loyalties if the pay is better. A friend of mine who felt God was moving him to a new company quickly found his coworkers canceling their scheduled lunch appointments with him as word of his resignation spread. Supposed friends turned ambivalent and even hostile overnight. *Men will transgress for a loaf of bread* (Proverbs 28:21).

David had enemies, but he also had allies. I would argue that the allies he developed sustained him when enemies were hunting him down. David was never alone because bloodstained allies rallied to him during his most vulnerable, desperate time. They were men who identified with and loved what David stood for—the heart of God.

They were a company of the vulnerable, the discontented, and those in distress and in debt. These were not the well-off, successful, and gainfully employed. David had more of a gang than an army,

> David therefore departed from there and escaped to the cave of Adullam. So when his brothers and all his father's house heard it, they went down there to him. And everyone who was in distress, everyone who was in debt, and everyone who was discontented gathered to him. So he became captain over them.
> *1 Samuel 22:1-2*

What is it that draws these men to David? Why do they come? Samuel writes to emphasize their desperate state—they were malcontents, failures, desperate. What's curious is that they are men who can identify with David. The allies of Adullam are men just like David. They get it. They understand his plight.

But just days before, they would've never identified with anything about him. This blessed son of Jesse; rock star; Goliath-slaying world champion; son-in-law to the king of Israel. There was nothing about David these bankrupt, indebted thieves could have related to. But now, David suddenly becomes one of them.

David is one of them. He has nothing. He has lost everything. He is in distress, in debt, and discontented. David is the captain of all their problems, all they've lost. David would never have picked any of these guys at the pick-up baseball game a week ago. But now, his life is their life.

That's what allies are: Men who are vulnerable and broken … together! Allies are a group of ragamuffin men who love each other. The allies at Adullam were a gang of beat-up men who knew they had nothing to bring to the table in and of themselves. A bystander would have said they were nothing.

But they have everything! Allies are men who are mutually desperate for God, for a Captain, for a purpose. The allies of Adullam know David has what they need. There is something about him they all long for. They want David because David wants God!

This is what we all need—allies of Adullam. We desperately need men who will rally to the love of God as brothers. We were made for relationship. We men have spent our lives running from such men. We have been told all our lives that being a man's man is to be independent, self-made, lone rangers that can handle any problem on our own. What a lie! It doesn't work; it's never worked.

Covenantal Friendship

Friendship is one of the most undervalued parts of our Christian walk. We have never been taught that friendship is a key part of growth as disciples. I would argue that we cannot become true worshippers and warriors without deep friendships in our daily walk with Jesus. Eugene Peterson explains,

> Friendship is a much underestimated aspect of spirituality. It's every bit as significant as prayer and fasting. Like the sacramental use of water and bread and wine, friendship takes what's common in human experience and turns it into something holy.[69]

The covenant of friendship is holy before the Lord. David had the men in the cave and Jonathan. Jesus had Peter, James, and John. Paul had Barnabas and Timothy. The spirituality of friendship is only forged in difficulty and hardship. Such friendship is only formed under such circumstances. It is in battles that true comrades are transformed from common relationships into covenant friendship.

I discovered this in my life under similar circumstances. Not unlike David, I lost the friends I had depended on, and the church I had built from the basement of my home to one of the largest churches in Colorado Springs. Due to circumstances I didn't fully understand, God began to move my life in a new direction. I resigned from the church I had known for twenty years and I found myself all alone. Or so I thought.

But as I retreated to my country home, away from the crowds and the church I loved, in a time of soul searching, a new group of people who loved me and Liz rallied to our side. During a desperate time of prayer, fasting, and seeking God for forty days, a group of men who identified with my plight formed around my seeking heart. My family and this group of people we barely knew came to our cave of Adullam. We prayed together, cried together, and shared our hearts.

These allies of Adullam came from all parts of the city. For months we sat by the fire, talked, and wept. What started as common-interest acquaintances gradually grew into covenant friends. These men gave me back my courage, my faith, and my heart. It was through these covenant friendships that a new church was birthed.

Covenant in Christ

All of us need bloodstained allies, covenantal friendships. But this covenant can only be formed and sustained under the rubric of a covenantal relationship with Jesus. Jesus must guide the relational connection through His power and grace. I would argue that such friendships only come through struggle, brokenness, and desperation. Desperation births covenant, and the only covenant that works is a covenant under the rule and love of Jesus. We open up and become vulnerable to our sin and sense of failure beneath the forgiveness and grace of God.

During Adolph Hitler's rise to power in the 1930s, Dietrich Bonhoeffer formed a group of men around himself for support, prayer, and mutual encouragement. All of these men were determined not to acquiesce to the hatred and brutality of the Brown Shirts and Nazi propaganda.

Aware of the ever-watchful eye of the Nazi SS, they retreated into a clandestine community to build a community of Christian love and support. Dr. Bonhoeffer became their captain, and they formed a new kind of seminary based on Scripture and covenantal relationships. This group eventually grew into The Confessing Church, a protest against the compromised Lutheran Church. It was built less around a doctrinal statement, though this was important, but rather the person and love of Jesus Christ. In his beautiful work on true Christian friendships, Bonhoeffer explains,

> Christianity means community through Jesus Christ and in Jesus Christ. No Christian community is more or less than this. Whether it be brief … or the daily fellowship of years, Christian community is this. We belong to one another only through and in Jesus Christ. What does this mean? It means, first, that a Christian needs others because of Jesus Christ. It means, second, that a Christian comes to others only through Jesus Christ. It means, third, that in Jesus Christ we have been chosen from eternity, accepted in time, and united for eternity.[70]

The physical presence of covenantal friendships is sacred. It is a source of joy and peace that strengthens our inner man. The imprisoned Apostle Paul, in the last days of his life, addresses Timothy as his "dearly beloved son in the faith." He remembers Timothy's tears when they parted for the last time (1 Timothy 1:2-4). Remembering the friends in the church at Thessalonica, Paul prays "night and day ... exceedingly that we might see your face" (1 Thessalonians 3:10). The Apostle John, well into his 90s, understands that his joy will be made full only by seeing his Christian brothers face to face (2 John 12). Jesus, knowing His time of torture and death was about to come, said to His most beloved friends, Peter, James, and John, "My soul is exceedingly sorrowful, even to death. Stay here and watch with Me" (Matthew 26:38).

We all need the physical presence of covenanted friends. God gave us physical bodies; Jesus came to us in a physical body. Our bodies are sacred temples of the Holy Spirit, and when we share in physical presence, we abide in the mutual Christ of whom we all share. Man was created from the beginning to not be alone, to need friendship. Jesus needed it. We all need it.

Under the grace of Christ, we are covenanted to His redemption and His presence. Being in the presence of brothers who are in the presence of Christ, we are strengthened and encouraged. The presence of Jesus in others becomes a source of the presence of God in our lives.

Real Presence

As a pastor I am often confronted with a statement that goes something like this: "Look, pastor, I don't need the church. I love Jesus and that's good enough for me. Why should I go to church and deal with all the problems of those people?"

It's a good question. For many, their experience in the church and in groups with other Christians has been anything but pleasant. The backbiting and gossip seems to be worse among supposed Christians than among their unchurched colleagues. The judgmental atmosphere of accountability groups has driven many a good man away from the church.

WORSHIPPER WARRIOR

What we are doing in our churches in the way of "fellowship" is, for the most part, not helpful. This is precisely why men are not growing deeper in their faith. It is why churches constantly split and so many are opting out of organized religion. I'm not advocating a better way of doing the same thing, but rather a completely new way of building relationships. I have come to believe in my study of Scripture and through personal experience that covenantal friendships can only be formed in the battles of real life, with real honesty, real vulnerability, and a covenantal commitment to Christ.

Men, we must have men in our lives that we can trust—and trust is only built through the fight of life under a covenantal intimate love for Jesus Christ. It is only through experiencing intimacy and wholehearted love for Christ that we can truly have intimacy and wholehearted love for our brothers. When Jesus tied the two together it was revolutionary—and it's revolutionary today. Jesus was explaining the purpose of the Christian life when He said,

> *'You shall love the Lord your God with all your heart, with all your soul, and with all your mind.' This is the first and great commandment. And the second is like it: 'You shall love your neighbor as yourself.' On these two commandments hang all the Law and the Prophets."*
> **Matthew 22:37-40**

Jesus is up to something. He is saying that the entire Bible, all of the prophets, all Christianity, hangs on this one statement! If it doesn't work in real presence with real men, then Jesus is a liar. But if it's true, we are in for an adventure by testing it! Real presence is real living, and real living is the honesty and heart sharing that we were created to experience.

For men to get real with men in real presence is the covenantal relationship. David found it in a desert cave and it saved his life. Paul found it in a prison cell in Rome and it gave him faith. John found it exiled on an island in the Aegean Sea and it brought him joy. Dietrich Bonhoeffer discovered it in threatening and catastrophic times and it gave him hope.

All of us need allies in our lives. Such allies are the foundation for our covenantal growth in Christ and with each other. Covenantal friendships are formed through real battles with real men who have a real and growing covenantal relationship with Christ. Let's ask God to bring such men into our lives.

The Dangerous Excursion: Day 9

1. In your opinion, why do we need allies in our lives as men?

2. In your opinion, what makes a bloodstained ally?

3. In your life, do you have any men with whom you can be completely real and vulnerable? If so who? If not, begin to ask God for such men.

4. Why not invite some men into a deeper covenantal relationship? Ask them to read this chapter and set up a time and place to discuss its contents. Time and place:

DAY 10: WILDERNESS

1 Samuel 23

18 And David stayed in strongholds in the wilderness, and remained in the mountains in the Wilderness of Ziph. Saul sought him every day, but God did not deliver him into his hand... And David stayed in the woods...

19 Then the Ziphites came up to Saul at Gibeah, saying, "Is David not hiding with us in strongholds in the woods, in the hill of Hachilah, which is on the south of Jeshimon? 20 Now therefore, O king, come down according to all the desire of your soul to come down; and our part shall be to deliver him into the king's hand."

21 And Saul said, "Blessed are you of the Lord, for you have compassion on me. 22 Please go and find out for sure, and see the place where his hideout is, and who has seen him there. For I am told he is very crafty. 23 See therefore, and take knowledge of all the lurking places where he hides; and come back to me with certainty, and I will go with you. And it shall be, if he is in the land, that I will search for him throughout all the clans of Judah."

24 So they arose and went to Ziph before Saul. But David and his men were in the Wilderness of Maon, in the plain on the south of Jeshimon. 25 When Saul and his men went to seek him, they told David. Therefore he went down to the rock, and stayed in the Wilderness of Maon. And when Saul heard that, he pursued David in the Wilderness of Maon. 26 Then Saul went on one side of the mountain, and David and his men on the other side of the mountain. So David made haste to get away from Saul, for Saul and his men were encircling David and his men to take them.

In describing God, C.S. Lewis once said, "He's wild, you know!" We are uncomfortable with God being wild, because a wild God is a free God. Richard Rohr writes, "God is always initiator, always good, always available, and the flow is always free."[71] We are threatened by such a free God because such freedom, such wildness, can't be manipulated or controlled.

To be unable to manipulate and control is not the preferred position of men. We value stability, power, and being in control of everything. We want to control our jobs, our wives, our hobbies, and our future. We have grown to believe that the more in control we are, the happier we will be. But it never quite works out. Control freaks like me aren't happier; we are just more uptight.

God is wild, and God is in control. He is utterly free. He is control of our lives, and He is working something deeper in us, something more profound through us, than we might want to know. This is the wildness of God. He is not going to be controlled by you or me.

Think about just how wild and free God is. He chooses Abraham and tells him to leave his country, his family, and his connections and go to the desert. He tells him he will be the father of a great nation through his son, but he doesn't allow his wife to get pregnant until she's over one hundred years old? That's so weird! Then as soon as things are working out, he tells Abraham to kill his son! Richard Rohr comments, "This has nothing to do with order, certitude, clarity, reason, logic, church authority or merit! This is an utterly free God trying to create spiritually free people."[72] God wants us to be free and God-wild. God's freedom is always flowing toward us. God's wildness is our redemption. God's freedom is our liberty.

The wild God of the Bible seems to do His most profound work in the wild. God-wild people are formed in God-wild places. The training camp of God is often the wilderness. It's no mistake that the root of the word "wilderness" is wild. God took Moses out of civilized Egypt to the wilderness, where He called him out to a greater work. Jacob also found God in the wild.

John the Baptizer was a wild man formed in the wilderness. History says he left his parents at fourteen and lived the rest of his life in the wilderness. Jesus went to the wilderness to be baptized by John, and was led by the Spirit into the wilds of Galilee to fast and pray. It was in the mountains and desert that Christ first faced off with Satan. The biblical MO of a free and wild God in forming a free man is that He seems to prefer the wilderness. Wilderness is mentioned hundreds of times in the Bible. The Old Testament is a field manual on wilderness living. Indeed, the wilderness is the backdrop of virtually every book.

Desperation

When we look at the whole of the Bible, we might be reminded that "nice" is never found. God's not building nice men, but rather men who are formed through wilderness living. In writing about John the Baptist, Mark's description sounds more like the nineteenth-century Jeremiah Johnson than the twenty-first-century metro male: "Now John was clothed with camel's hair and with a leather belt around his waist, and he ate locusts and wild honey."[73] John's entire persona has been formed by the wilderness—he looks like the wilderness, he smells like the wilderness, his appetites are formed by the wilderness.

David also finds himself in the wilderness. Pushed out by Saul, on the run with a bounty on his head, David has no place to go *but* the wilderness. "And David stayed in strongholds in the wilderness and remained in the mountains in the Wilderness of Ziph. Saul sought him every day, but God did not deliver him into his hand."[74] David, who had been called out of the hills of Bethlehem to the palace of Saul, is now back in the haunts he had grown to know so well. David is in the wilderness, and he will be further formed by it over the next decade.

With no home but the mountains, forest, and caves of Israel—and even, for a while, Philistia—David will live a nomadic existence. His band of men will grow and the responsibilities of carrying a growing village of families will add to the pressure. But with no place to lay his head, David will experience what his Savior would come to know so well a thousand years later: David is now a wilderness man.

The natural wilderness prophesies of the spiritual wilderness. Many times in my life I have experienced wilderness seasons. Some have called it the "dark night of the soul," or "the valley." Martin Luther, the great reformer, described such times as *anfechtungen,* German for "deep spiritual depression." Historian David Steinmetz describes the terror Luther experienced in those times as a fear that "God had turned his back on him once and for all," abandoning him "to suffer the pains of hell."[75] All of us face times when it feels like God has forsaken us and the dark clouds of hopelessness are raining their anxious drops upon our hearts. Some of the symptoms of the wilderness in our lives might be:

- A sense of deep loss and abandonment; loss of a job, divorce, betrayal
- A feeling of God's absence
- A lack of desire for seeking God in prayer, reading the Word, and worship
- Utter hopelessness
- More intense battles with fleshly temptations
- Loss of joy and peace
- Struggles with anger, frustration, and depression

It is in such times that I believe God does His most powerful work. I have come to believe from Scripture, counseling, and personal experience that the wilderness is God's boot camp for building men. It is in the spiritual topography of the wilderness that God develops a new set of convictions and trust. It is a place of God's discipline. One author describes it well:

> The wilderness is a place of desperation, of being lost, of darkness. It is a place where we die again and again; where we stumble and feel we will never rise. It is the place where all of our illusions of self-sufficiency and self-righteousness are stripped away, showing our naked sinful selves. In the wilderness the veneer of meaning is stripped away. Here we fall into the abyss of chaos and beyond, into a deeper abyss of God's mysterious love. In the wilderness we meet the devil in a thousand forms who tempts us and torments us. We meet ourselves as enemy and friend. We encounter God in a combat of opposing wills.[76]

David must now trust God like never before. He is no longer the great warrior on the battlefield coming home to adoring crowds, but rather the renegade outlaw returning to nothing! He has no home! He has been stripped of all dignity and respect. His only friends are the bloodstained allies of Adullam and God.

Fortress

God and David. David and God. In the wilderness. A new relationship; a new man is being cultivated in the caves and valleys of the Israeli desert. What is most striking about this time in David's life is how often the Bible uses the terms "fortress" and "wilderness" almost interchangeably. The Ziphites, in betraying David to Saul, explain, *"Is David not hiding with us in the strongholds in the woods?"*[77] In response, Saul says something interesting: *"See therefore, and take knowledge of all the lurking places where he hides."*[78] I have been in the wilderness of Israel and it's amazing how many caves, valleys, and hidden places there are.

Once, while staying near the Dead Sea, my son and I went out late at night to explore the Wilderness of Engedi, the stronghold of David in Psalm 24. This is where the Jewish guerrillas took refuge during the revolts of A.D. 66 and 70. The great stronghold of Masada is just south of this area. In all probability, that's where David encamped many times.

In the wilderness, one's perceptions change. In the complete silence of the desert, your sight, hearing, and sense of smell sharpen. With no distractions, one's senses are heightened. In the tradition of spirituality, there have always been the mystical writings of the desert fathers and those who found God in the wilderness. Eugene Peterson writes, "Everybody— at least everybody who has anything to do with God—spends time in the wilderness."[79] David hasn't chosen the wilderness; it has chosen him.

God has chased David into the wilderness. It is in the desperation of the wilderness that David discovers God as his strength, his rock, and his fortress. As far as I can tell in studying the Psalms, there is no other time where David so cultivates this kind of deep intimacy in the protection and love of God as in the desperation of living in the wilderness. Psalm 18 expresses the heart of David, and the subscript gives us the wilderness context, *"To the Chief Musician, a Psalm of David the servant of the LORD, who spoke to the LORD the words of this song on the day that the LORD delivered him from the hand of all his enemies and the hand of Saul."* This certainly could be speaking of the context in 1 Samuel 23-24. Let me summarize David's prayer,

> *I will love You, O LORD, my strength,*
> *The LORD is my rock and my fortress and my deliverer;*
> *My God, my strength, in whom I will trust;*
> *My shield and the horn of my salvation, my stronghold.*
> *I will call upon the LORD, who is worthy to be praised,*
> *So shall I be saved from my enemies ...*
> *He delivered me from my strong enemy, from those who hated me,*
> *For they were too strong for me ...*
> *For by You I can run against a troop,*
> *By my God I can leap over a wall ...*
> *He teaches my hands to make war,*
> *So that my arms can bend a bow of bronze ...*
> *For you have armed me with strength for the battle.*
> **Psalm 18:1-39**

Do you see what's happening to David? He is being formed into a warrior through battles in the desert. His heart is changing and being transformed through the desperation of the wilderness. David has no palace walls, no armor, no mighty army to back him up. He has no appointments to keep, deadlines to meet, or assignments to complete. David is alone with God. David knows God must be his fortress. The Lord is becoming his strength, and he is being formed into a new kind of warrior. David's heart is being honed and chiseled by God through the desperation of the wilderness. He has never known such weakness. And he has never needed God so desperately.

> *The pangs of death surrounded me,*
> *And the floods of ungodliness made me afraid.*
> *The sorrows of sheol surrounded me;*
> *The snares of death confronted me.*
> *In my distress I called upon the LORD,*
> *And cried out to my God;*
> *He heard my voice from His temple ...*
> *He sent out His arrows and scattered the foe."*
> **Psalm 18:4-5, 14**

David is learning to cry out on a whole new level. This is a Psalm not unlike many others where David cries out for help, desperate for God's deliverance—most of which are written in the wilderness. David is discovering the God who answers prayer when death itself is knocking at the door. David feels the reality of the sorrows of Hell confronting his heart.

God has led David into the wilderness. He is stripping him of his self-sufficiency, his dependence on his innate abilities and talents. God is bringing David into the heart of trusting Him. Trust is only built through desperation. David's trust in God is being honed in the spiritual boot camp of the crevices of the wilderness.

The Battleground

The wilderness is a battleground. It is the place where we are under constant attack with no clear directive on what to do. We feel alone, and we feel insecure. The wilderness of the soul can be a time of desperation and sorrow.

I have a friend who has navigated a life full of successes. A seemingly endless stream of accolades has followed his career; he's a former college president who now has a national speaking ministry. But one day last year, he came home to discover email traffic on his wife's computer that indicated an inappropriate relationship with another man. As the affair was exposed, this man was thrown from the highest echelons of success into the wilderness of his soul in just a few days. For the next year, instead of accepting speaking engagements, he was setting up counseling appointments.

His marriage became the wilderness battleground as he fought for his wife, his kids, and his heart. All of us will experience times in our lives when God thrusts us into the wilderness. The wilderness will be a testing ground of our heart, a place where we will face decisions of our will that will determine the future state of our heart.

We will be faced with a fight for our integrity. Either pressing into God and His love and praising Him for the deeper work He is developing within, or cursing God and running from the discipline and boot camp of our hearts. The choice is ours. The test is from God.

The wild and free God is forming wild and free men. He is not building nice men, but wilderness men. Freedom comes through the wilderness. God is building into you a man who is rugged of heart and compassionate of soul. The wilderness is His training ground.

The Dangerous Excursion: Day 10

1. How would you define "the wilderness"?

2. What is the purpose of the wilderness?

3. Have you ever gone through a wilderness time? Are you currently in a wilderness time? If so, what has/is God teaching you?

DAY 11: INQUIRY

1 Samuel 23

1 Then they told David, saying, "Look, the Philistines are fighting against Keilah, and they are robbing the threshing floors."

2 Therefore David inquired of the Lord, saying, "Shall I go and attack these Philistines?"

And the Lord said to David, "Go and attack the Philistines, and save Keilah."

3 But David's men said to him, "Look, we are afraid here in Judah. How much more then if we go to Keilah against the armies of the Philistines?" 4 Then David inquired of the Lord once again.

And the Lord answered him and said, "Arise, go down to Keilah. For I will deliver the Philistines into your hand." 5 And David and his men went to Keilah and fought with the Philistines, struck them with a mighty blow, and took away their livestock. So David saved the inhabitants of Keilah.

6 Now it happened, when Abiathar the son of Ahimelech fled to David at Keilah, that he went down with an ephod in his hand.

7 And Saul was told that David had gone to Keilah. So Saul said, "God has delivered him into my hand, for he has shut himself in by entering a town that has gates and bars." 8 Then Saul called all the people together for war, to go down to Keilah to besiege David and his men.

9 When David knew that Saul plotted evil against him, he said to Abiathar the priest, "Bring the ephod here." 10 Then David said, "O Lord God of Israel, Your servant has certainly heard that Saul seeks to come to Keilah to destroy the city for my sake. 11 Will the men of Keilah deliver me into his hand? Will Saul come down, as Your servant has heard? O Lord God of Israel, I pray, tell Your servant."

And the Lord said, "He will come down."

12 Then David said, "Will the men of Keilah deliver me and my men into the hand of Saul?"

And the Lord said, "They will deliver you."

13 So David and his men, about six hundred, arose and departed from Keilah and went wherever they could go. Then it was told Saul that David had escaped from Keilah; so he halted the expedition.

Every fall I go on a journey with my sons into the wilderness of Colorado. We affectionately call it the Roosevelt Camp, naming it after Teddy Roosevelt, without whose foresight no wilderness lands would still exist in this country. Officially, it's an elk hunt, but unofficially it is my time alone with God to seek His heart, to converse, to unburden my life. Every year I encounter God in the forests of the Flattop Wilderness.

What I love most about it is the stillness. No distractions, no noise, no people. No cell phone coverage is the best part! Granted, we set up camp and there is the noise of our preparations and conversations around the fire. There are other camps near us. But when we strap on the boots, put on the backpack, sling on the rifle, and walk into the dark forest at four-thirty a.m., the spiritual journey begins. Finding my spot as the stars blaze overhead, the wilderness becomes a sacred place of inquiry—a sanctuary of prayer and seeking.

I have chosen the wilderness as a sacred place of inquiry. David didn't; he was chased into the wilderness. Chosen by God to be king, anointed by the great prophet Samuel at the age of thirteen, his teen years were spent in the court of King Saul. He was loved as a singer and musician. He saved Israel from a Philistine assault and became a hero to the entire nation. But now, what has happened? He has been driven to the wilderness as an outlaw.

This just may be the lowest point in David's life.

What a man does in his lowest ebb is who he is. In graduate school, one of my professors was fond of saying, "Who you are in adversity is who you are." A man's heart is most revealed when the veneer is torn off. When all the accoutrements of life, religion, job, and accomplishment are stripped away, there stands the man, naked before his Creator, naked before himself. It is in such dark canyons of the soul that character and motives are forged and developed.

God is forming a wholehearted worshipper and warrior. God is making David into a king, a new kind of king. Not a king like Saul, but a wholehearted man of God—a man God can trust to shepherd His people. God's anvil will be the trouble that David is about to encounter. David will have to trust the Lord in a new way.

Unsure and Unstable

Acting on the advice of the prophet Gad, David leaves the shelter of Adullam to enter the desolation of the mountains and wilderness. Tidings have come to David of an eventual attack by the Philistines against the border town of Keilah. The farmers had just harvested their crops when the Philistines attacked and plundered their goods. The men of Keilah know David as a warrior and call out an SOS to him for help.

This is the first time in the Bible that we see David seeking God in prayer. Has he prayed before? Of course he has. The fact that David is called a man after God's own heart is testimony enough. His worship before Saul that drove back demons was a witness of the life of prayer that David has developed. I'm sure David sought God in prayer before entering the Valley of Elah. But this is the first time in Samuel's work that it is directly recorded that David "inquired of the Lord."

David is obviously unsure of a course of action. In times past, the events, circumstances, and situations have all been very clear. The actions needed were obvious. But this is quite different. David is not sure what he should do—should he take on the problems of Keilah and risk the lives of his few men? Should he move on and let Keilah deal with its own predicament? This really isn't his problem or his fight. What does God want him to do?

There are things in our life that are best answered through discussion with people. There are things in our life that can only be understood through study and research. But there are things from God—unsure and unstable circumstances—that can only be grasped through prayer and crying out to Him. The answer isn't clear. No one can answer the question but God. No advice or counsel is going to suffice; we need God's word directly to us. In such times, God's will can only be discerned through inquiring of Him directly.

There are times in our lives when all seems to be going well. The job is paying the bills, the wife has a home she can decorate, the kids are playing on their favorite teams and their grades are good. And then suddenly, we're beside ourselves, overwhelmed. We don't know what's going on within us or around us. We begin to call into question everything we believe in. There are eruptions at work, or radical changes in our marriage, and we are thrown off balance. Our emotions go topsy-turvy. We're not in control any more.

As terrible as it seems, as dangerous as the circumstances may feel, there is a beautiful work of God in the center of the storm. God is training us to inquire, to call out to Him. He is actually at work to create a lack of control in our life that will press us into inquiry, prayer, seeking.

David has to deal with God and allow God to deal with him. God is making David into the man He desires him to become. A true man. David is discovering his own humanity as he cries out to God. Eugene Peterson explains,

> What happens is that no matter what else David is doing, he's basically dealing with God; and the more he deals with God, the more human he becomes—the more he becomes "David." Holy is our best word to describe that life—the human aliveness that comes from dealing with God-Alive. We're most human when we deal with God.[80]

David is becoming wholehearted. He is becoming the David whom God can work through and use. When we deal with God in prayer, when we seek God for answers to the mysteries of our lives, we are being chiseled into wholehearted humans. Paul describes this in Romans 8:18-19: "For I consider the sufferings of this present time … for the earnest expectation of the revealing of the sons of God." God is revealing who we are through suffering. We were created for dealing with God and surrendering to His dealings with us. This is the building of a wholehearted worshipper.

Mysteries of God

We want to figure it all out. We as men, much more than women, struggle with feelings of being out of control. I know a young man in his early thirties who has just received his master's degree with top honors, who recently shared with me his plans for the future. Newly married, he has a well-paying job, and just bought a house. With a new healthy baby, all is flowing in the right direction for him. I smiled during our conversation—not just because I'm proud of him, which I am, but also because I know that "my will be done," often conflicts with "Thy will be done." He will go through many steps of discovery with God, and I want to be there for him as he does. But hard times will come, and this is how a man grows up.

Isaiah said it well: "My thoughts are nothing like your thoughts," says the LORD. "And my ways are far beyond anything you could imagine."[81] God is a mystery in His dealings with us. We are not too comfortable with the mysteries of God. We want certainty. We want God's "plans." We want to know that we win. Right? You know that's true. But God's ways and thoughts often conflict with ours.

I'm sure David was beginning to believe he led a charmed life. From sheep herder to rock star. From Bethlehem to the king's palace. From the family caterer to champion warrior. All in a couple of years!

And now this? Run out of town, fired, despised, and under siege. What's next? *God, what should I do?* David cries out. The instability of his situation, the mystery of God, is uncomfortable. In the West, we have been preoccupied with how much we know about God and have often neglected *how* we know the things we know about God. The how is neglected for the what.

God is doing a work within David. David must inquire. David must turn to God. David is learning to love God through prayer and inquiry. The mystery of God's will awaits the seeking heart. The mystery of God sets up a seeking heart. This just might be what Jesus was talking about when He said, *"Keep on asking, and you will receive what you ask for. Keep on seeking, and you will find. Keep on knocking, and the door will be opened to you. For everyone who asks, receives. Everyone who seeks, finds. And to everyone who knocks, the door will be opened."*[82] Jesus is promising that if we will keep on asking Him, seeking Him, knocking on the door of the mysteries of God, He will reveal His plan and His will to us. The secrets of the Lord are for the seeker.

But the process also matters. David is being transformed through seeking God. It is *how* David is being changed in the journey that is building a wholehearted worshipper and warrior.

Praying Afraid

Richard Rohr writes, "We ended up seeing holy things faintly, trying to understand Great Things with a whittled-down mind, and trying to love God with our small and divided heart. It has been like trying to view the galaxies with a $5 pair of binoculars."[83] Prayer can change this. David must learn; we must learn. Prayer molds the whole heart.

> And the Lord said to David, "Go and attack the Philistines, and save Keilah." But David's men said to him, "Look, we are afraid here in Judah. How much more then if we go to Keilah against the armies of the Philistines?" Then David inquired of the Lord once again.
> *1 Samuel 23:1-7*

I like to call such a situation "praying afraid." David seeks and hears from the Lord, but his men don't. Fear is all around. Fear is pervasive. This is a risky situation. It is no exaggeration to say David is cashing in his chips—all or nothing? Might it be better to stay bloodless? David doesn't have to take on this fight. Technically it's not his anyway! He is not The Protector of the Domain any longer. He can walk away.

But God has spoken to him! David inquired, and God spoke. The first word from God is "Go." The first two letters of God are "GO." Obedience usually means action. David must now act.

But David has never fought with these men by his side. Yes, he appreciates their willingness to follow him. Yes, he appreciates their companionship. But is this the best situation for learning how to fight together? Against the mighty Philistines? The sea people have the iron, the training camps, the seasoned warriors. Probably not the best environment to break in a bunch of farmers.

God is a mystery, and His ways often are more often counterintuitive than we would like to admit. David faces what every man must face if he desires to grow into wholehearted devotion—the mystery, the non-duality of God. Prayer is an exercise in keeping our heart and mind open long enough to see what God might be doing in His hidden ways.[84] David's men don't get it, and David is still unsure if *he* gets it. So, he does the right thing—he seeks God once again.

Our greatest critics will often be those who don't seek God in prayer. I'm not saying our critics don't seek God; I'm saying often they don't seek the Lord in prayer over the issues we are seeking and struggling with. I have come to believe God doesn't call most people to the same level of inquiry as He does the leader. The *leader* must inquire. The *leader* must not give up. The *leader* must hear from God in muddled circumstances.

David's men are afraid, and rightly so. David's men don't want this fight, and understandably so. But David has heard from God, and God has said, "go." David obeys, and God moves … powerfully and victoriously. The ways of God are a mystery, but the promises of God are sure. David is learning to be wary of men's opinions and to trust God's voice.

The wholehearted worshipper and warrior must inquire for his job, for his family, for his church, for his future. No one else can do it but him. He can seek advice and counsel, but ultimately when the smoke clears and the fog lifts, it is the man whom God has called that He speaks to.

God has called you to something. God has made you a leader somewhere. God has placed you in situations that are above your pay grade. He will lead you into danger that will be fearful at times. You will have people who are telling you what to do, how and when to do it, and you will have to seek God. You will have to inquire. You will have to inquire with your whole heart.

God will create situations in your life that will require you to seek Him in passionate prayer until you hear. Don't forget it is the *how,* not the *what,* that makes a man of God. God is forming you! God is fashioning you to look and smell like a man of the wilderness, a warrior, a man seasoned by the battles of prayer.

The Dangerous Excursion: Day 11

1. **Why does God place us in unsure circumstances?**

2. **Why are we as men so uncomfortable with the mysteries of God?**

3. **What is God doing in your life these days? How is He forming you into a wholehearted worshipper and warrior?**

DAY 12: COURAGE

Psalm 31

1 In You, O Lord, I put my trust;
   Let me never be ashamed;
   Deliver me in Your righteousness.
   2 Bow down Your ear to me,
   Deliver me speedily;
   Be my rock of refuge,
   A fortress of defense to save me.
3 For You are my rock and my fortress;
   Therefore, for Your name's sake,
   Lead me and guide me.
   4 Pull me out of the net which they have secretly laid for me,
   For You are my strength.
   5 Into Your hand I commit my spirit;
   You have redeemed me, O Lord God of truth.
6 I have hated those who regard useless idols;
   But I trust in the Lord.
   7 I will be glad and rejoice in Your mercy,
   For You have considered my trouble;
   You have known my soul in adversities,
   8 And have not shut me up into the hand of the enemy;
   You have set my feet in a wide place.
9 Have mercy on me, O Lord, for I am in trouble;
   My eye wastes away with grief,
   Yes, my soul and my body!
   10 For my life is spent with grief,
   And my years with sighing;
   My strength fails because of my iniquity,
   And my bones waste away.
   11 I am a reproach among all my enemies,
   But especially among my neighbors,
   And am repulsive to my acquaintances;
   Those who see me outside flee from me.
   12 I am forgotten like a dead man, out of mind;

I am like a broken vessel.
13 For I hear the slander of many;
Fear is on every side;
While they take counsel together against me,
They scheme to take away my life.
14 But as for me, I trust in You, O Lord;
I say, "You are my God."
15 My times are in Your hand;
Deliver me from the hand of my enemies,
And from those who persecute me.
16 Make Your face shine upon Your servant;
Save me for Your mercies' sake.
17 Do not let me be ashamed, O Lord, for I have called upon You;
Let the wicked be ashamed;
Let them be silent in the grave.
18 Let the lying lips be put to silence,
Which speak insolent things proudly and contemptuously against
the righteous.
19 Oh, how great is Your goodness,
Which You have laid up for those who fear You,
Which You have prepared for those who trust in You
In the presence of the sons of men!
20 You shall hide them in the secret place of Your presence
From the plots of man;
You shall keep them secretly in a pavilion
From the strife of tongues.
21 Blessed be the Lord,
For He has shown me His marvelous kindness in a strong city!
22 For I said in my haste,
"I am cut off from before Your eyes";
Nevertheless You heard the voice of my supplications
When I cried out to You.
23 Oh, love the Lord, all you His saints!
For the Lord preserves the faithful,
And fully repays the proud person.
24 Be of good courage,
And He shall strengthen your heart,
All you who hope in the Lord.

David is under siege from every direction. His troubles are mounting. He feels weak and is under duress. In one of his early poems, the besieged warrior poet pens these haunting words.

David feels the pressure on his heart. He feels broken. He is crying out to God and allowing his heart to be vulnerable. David is utterly honest about his feelings. He feels wrenching agony at the deepest levels of his soul. In this Psalm, "shame" is mentioned three times (verses 1 and 17). David makes a heart association with his troubles and the shame he is battling.

Shame and Weakness

New York Times bestselling author, blogger, and sociologist Dr. Brené Brown has written extensively on shame and vulnerability. She defines shame as:

> Basically the fear of being unlovable—it's the total opposite of owning our story and feeling worthy. In fact the definition of shame that I have developed from my research is: Shame is intensely painful feeling or experience of believing that we are flawed and therefore unworthy of love and belonging. Shame keeps worthiness away by convincing us that owning our stories will lead to people thinking less of us. Shame is all about fear.[85]

Brown has written that after ten thousand interviews, the shame area for women almost always centers around their looks and appearance, but for men, it is the fear of weakness. We as men wake up each day with the big questions: *Do I have what it takes to win? Am I strong enough?* Satan knows our weaknesses as men, and that is where he comes to steal our desires, kill our hearts, and destroy our masculinity.

I have seven children, most of them grown now, but as little men and women running and playing around our house, the differences between them, based on gender, was startling. With four boys and three girls, my anecdotal R&D would support Dr. Brown's conclusions. I can say unequivocally that my wife and I never had one of our sons ask for makeup, want to paint his nails, or play dress-up. But we certainly had our share of issues related to who had the biggest muscles and who was the most accurate on our shooting range.

God made men to be warriors and protectors. I have watched our sons stand up to some surly characters in protecting our home and watching over their sisters. Once, when I was under siege with a death threat for an uncompromising stand on an issue, my son asked if he could guard our gate with a shotgun. He was only sixteen, but I loved his courage.

So, it goes without saying that the wound of Satan upon a man will be his strength. The reality of or even the perception of weakness will be a shame area for every man.

Vulnerability

David is in the wilderness, both geographically and spiritually. His heart is feeling both temptation and pain. He is being bombarded by conflicting feelings and thoughts. But in Psalm 31, we see a man of courage, a man willing to be honest, a man willing to be vulnerable.

David is open and honest before God. He is making a conscious effort to fight shame by being vulnerable with his Lord. David is breaking the power of Satan and the power of shame by trusting God. Interestingly, Brené Brown says the key to wholehearted living is vulnerability.

> If we want to live and love with our whole hearts, and if we want to engage with the world from a place of worthiness, we have to talk about the things that get in the way—especially shame, fear, and vulnerability.[86]

In her TED talk on the subject, she admits that the main thing separating those who continue to live in shame and those who go on to live wholehearted lives is what she calls "excruciating vulnerability."[87] David is being vulnerable at the core of his heart. He is not allowing the enemy to win the battle for it.

The greatest fight in any man's life is the battle of the heart.

There is a battle going on between shame and trust, and David is choosing trust. David's courage is the component we must all cultivate. It takes courage to fight for our heart. It takes courage not to give in to the old scripting of our thinking that echoes through our minds: *You are a loser, you always give up when things get tough, you are a weakling and a sucker. You DON'T have what it takes. You're an idiot.*

We often think of courage as being heroic and doing something that sacrifices for others in a dangerous situation. But the root of the word "courage" is *cor*—Latin for "heart."[88] In its original context, courage meant, "To speak one's mind by telling one's heart."[89] Courage is heroic, but not in the ways we have grown accustomed to seeing. The courage I'm talking about is the vulnerability we observe in David—trusting God through openness and honesty about who we are and the feelings we are experiencing. Heroism is often about putting our lives on the line, but courage is about putting our hearts on the line.

To grow us into wholehearted men, God wants to cultivate honesty and vulnerability in our hearts. Instead of running from our fears and failures, we must learn to run *to* them. Instead of *covering* up our shame, we must *open* up *to* our shame. Instead of posing and pretending to be strong, we must be honest and open *about* our weakness. This takes courage.

Heart Attack

Most men in their adult years have heart attacks. Not the physical kind—the spiritual kind. The enemy has taken us out through continual, unrelenting heart attacks. We fear facing our wounds, fear dealing with our shame.

The Apostle Paul, often called "the Apostle of the heart set free," spoke of this dilemma in his writings. In dealing with shame, Paul wrote,

> *Therefore, since through God's mercy we have this ministry, we do not lose heart. Rather, we have renounced secret and shameful ways; we do not use deception, nor do we distort the word of God. On the contrary, by setting forth the truth plainly we commend ourselves to everyone's conscience in the sight of God.*
> **2 Corinthians 4:2**

Paul is saying the prescription to the attacks upon our hearts is to commend ourselves to God and men. We commend ourselves to the hearts of other men. We commend ourselves to God. We open up to our shame, our weakness, our hurt, and we trust God to heal us through vulnerability and openness. The alternative is the loss of our heart!

Most men today are living half-heartedly. They have lost a part of their heart to shame and are unwilling to face the darkness. Fear grips their hearts and thus, they have lost touch with part of it. The results in our society are devastating. Men with half chests who can't stand for anything, give in to everything! We have no battles to fight because we have no hearts to fight with. Ours is a culture of emasculated men who are confused and weak.

Preach to Yourself

But men, in facing our shame, facing our weakness, we actually get set free! It's counterintuitive but courageous. C.S. Lewis captured our dilemma by writing,

> If there lurks in most modern minds the notion that to desire our own good and earnestly to hope for the enjoyment of it is a bad thing, I submit that this notion has crept in from Kant and the Stoics and is no part of the Christian faith. Indeed, if we consider the unblushing promises of reward and the staggering nature of the rewards promised in the Gospels, it would seem that Our Lord finds our desires not too strong, but too weak. We are half-hearted creatures, fooling about with drink and sex and ambition when infinite joy is offered us, like an ignorant child who wants to go on making mud pies in a slum because he cannot imagine what is meant by the offer of a holiday at the sea. We are far too easily pleased.[90]

Yes, I am far too easily pleased most of the time. It's the story of our lives. Easily pleased and missing out on the joy of wholehearted living. It will take wholehearted courage to face our sin, to face our weakness, to face our shame. The route to wholehearted joy is courage.

It will take courage to seek out our own good, that which we long for. For far too long we have not trusted our heart because we have seen the devastation that it brings us. But that was your old heart, your old scripting, and your old habits.

Now you have a new heart. To long for our good is not selfish but courageous. But how can we do that? How can I seek my own good without becoming selfish? It all goes back to the heart God has given you.

WORSHIPPER WARRIOR

As a worshipper of Jesus, as a warrior with Jesus, you've now been given a fresh, new, sensitive heart. New desires course through your spiritual veins. It's why you are reading this book.

Trust Jesus with your new whole heart. Trust that God is taking you on a journey and that through the power of the Holy Spirit within you, you can—yes, you *can*—face your greatest and deepest fears. Through a new powerful walk with God, you can face the shame of your childhood, the wounds inflicted by men, and become a new kind of man.

David's courage is wrapped up in a robust trust. He trusts that God will see him through even as he lives in caves, eats berries in the wilderness, and is constantly on the run as an outlaw. In this poem, David takes twenty-two verses to share with great vulnerability his heart and shame before God. But now he preaches, as it were, to himself. He reminds himself why he will make it and how he will find courage to continue. David finishes out his poem with a fresh courage:

> *Oh, love the Lord, all you His saints!*
> *For the Lord preserves the faithful,*
> *And fully repays the proud person.*
> *Be of good courage,*
> *And He shall strengthen your heart,*
> *All you who hope in the LORD.*
> **Psalm 31:23-24**

David's courage stems from his intimate knowledge that God will pull him through his dark night of the soul. What I love most about David is his honesty, even about his enemies. David feels vulnerable and he wants justice. He is confident that God will "fully repay the proud person." Such honesty is courageous.

But more than anything else, David encourages himself that God will strengthen his heart. David is the first full-fledged, wholehearted worshipper and warrior. He is a type of what we seek to become. He is speaking to himself of what he wants to be.

Preach to yourself today. Speak to your heart and tell it what you believe to be true—the bad and the good. Be open and honest. Don't be afraid anymore. Shun fear through a robust, gutsy, gritty prayer to God. With all the grit God has put within you, write a poem to Him. Tell him how you feel, what you fear, and then, with the acrimony and passion of your heart, give it all to Him. Be honest and tell Jesus how you feel.

But don't miss this—let Him know you will trust Him through the pain, the shame, the hardships. Tell the Lord that you will not quit. Express in your own words a trust that He will empower you be a wholehearted worshipper, a wholehearted warrior!

The Dangerous Excursion, Day 12:

Write out your own poem, your own psalm, expressing your commitment to breaking the power of shame with the courage of your new heart:

DAY 13: REFUGE

1 Samuel 26

1 Now the Ziphites came to Saul at Gibeah, saying, "Is David not hiding in the hill of Hachilah, opposite Jeshimon?" 2 Then Saul arose and went down to the Wilderness of Ziph, having three thousand chosen men of Israel with him, to seek David in the Wilderness of Ziph. 3 And Saul encamped in the hill of Hachilah, which is opposite Jeshimon, by the road. But David stayed in the wilderness, and he saw that Saul came after him into the wilderness. 4 David therefore sent out spies, and understood that Saul had indeed come.

5 So David arose and came to the place where Saul had encamped. And David saw the place where Saul lay, and Abner the son of Ner, the commander of his army. Now Saul lay within the camp, with the people encamped all around him. 6 Then David answered, and said to Ahimelech the Hittite and to Abishai the son of Zeruiah, brother of Joab, saying, "Who will go down with me to Saul in the camp?" And Abishai said, "I will go down with you."

7 So David and Abishai came to the people by night; and there Saul lay sleeping within the camp, with his spear stuck in the ground by his head. And Abner and the people lay all around him. 8 Then Abishai said to David, "God has delivered your enemy into your hand this day. Now therefore, please, let me strike him at once with the spear, right to the earth; and I will not have to strike him a second time!"

9 But David said to Abishai, "Do not destroy him; for who can stretch out his hand against the Lord's anointed, and be guiltless?" 10 David said furthermore, "As the Lord lives, the Lord shall strike him, or his day shall come to die, or he shall go out to battle and perish. 11 The Lord forbid that I should stretch out my hand against the Lord's anointed. But please, take now the spear and the jug of water that are by his head, and let us go." 12 So David took the spear and the jug of water by Saul's head, and they got away; and no man saw or knew it or awoke. For they were all asleep, because a deep sleep from the Lord had fallen on them ...

22 And David said, "Here is the king's spear. Let one of the young men come over and get it. 23 May the Lord repay every man for his righteousness and his faithfulness; for the Lord delivered you into my hand today, but I would not stretch out my hand against the Lord's anointed. 24 And indeed, as your life was valued much this day in my eyes, so let my life be valued much in the eyes of the Lord, and let Him deliver me out of all tribulation."

25 Then Saul said to David, "May you be blessed, my son David! You shall both do great things and also still prevail."

A spear in the hand of a trained and seasoned warrior was an instrument to be feared. As far back as archeological and anthropological studies have gone, one finds the spear being used for hunting and warfare. It probably originated in Africa and was an important weapon in the Nubian and ancient Egyptian military forces. The spear may be the ancestor of such weaponry as the lance, pilum, bill, and pike. Some believe the spear or lance later gave rise to the bow and arrow. In current military gear, the influence of the spear can be seen in the rifle-mounted bayonet.

With the coming of the Bronze Age and the military innovations of the Philistines, the spear became the go-to weapon of the Israelites. The head, armed with flint, obsidian, iron, steel, or bronze, could be shaped and chiseled into a deadly, razor-sharp cutting edge. (Because of the serrated edges, I have used obsidian for skinning large-game animals.) Like a bullet, a spear in the hand of a trained warrior gave him the ability to kill from a remarkable distance.

Saul carried a spear wherever he went. He even had it by his side when he listened to David playing music. Saul used it, too—not just for waging physical battles, but also for fighting relational battles. Saul's spear was not only aimed at his enemies on a battlefield, but at his "friends" in the palace.

The Art of Spear Throwing

As David's popularity grew, Saul's grip on his spear tightened. The demonic spirit over him grew stronger as his paranoia of David deepened. The spear became Saul's refuge for dealing with David.

And it happened on the next day that the distressing spirit from God came upon Saul, and he prophesied inside the house. So

David played music with his hand, as at other times; but there was a spear in Saul's hand. And Saul cast the spear, for he said, "I will pin David to the wall!" But David escaped his presence twice.
1 Samuel 18:10-11

David becomes an outlaw and runs for his life. But he doesn't *have* to. David could choose to become a spear-thrower just like Saul. After all, Saul is his mentor in kingly ways, Kingdom rulership, anointed leadership. It seems altogether remarkable that David doesn't take up spear-throwing.

What should a man do when someone throws spears at him? Isn't it natural to return the compliment? Spear-throwing is what real men do. You don't just put up with it and run. How unmanly, unwarriorlike, is that? Shouldn't David have just taken that spear out of the wall and pinned Saul to his couch? Gene Edwards comments,

> And in doing this small feat of returning thrown spears, you will prove many things: You are courageous. You stand for the right. You boldly stand against the wrong. You are tough and can't be pushed around. You will not stand for injustice or unfair treatment. You are a defender of the faith, keeper of the flame, detector of all heresy. You will not be wronged. All of these attributes then combine to prove that you are also, obviously, a candidate for kingship. Yes, perhaps you are the Lord's anointed.[91]

David never learned the art of throwing a spear. He didn't even consider throwing the spear back. It might be that his friends and advisors at the time would have counseled him to stand up for his himself and not be a sissy but a real man—why not just pick up the spear and throw it back? *Stand up for yourself, David!*

The Order of Refuge

But David was not of the order of Saul, not one of the spear-throwing leaders. David's refuge was not found in being an accomplished javelin thrower, but in a trust of God that didn't require a spear. David was of the order of God. He was growing in being a different type of warrior through growing deeper as a worshipper.

David is now on the run, hiding in caves, looking for crevices and crags for escape routes. Each day is a challenge to evade Saul and keep a grip on his own growing army. But such challenges pale in comparison to the test God has awaiting him.

Saul is unarmed, unprotected, and asleep at David's feet.

With one thrust of a spear or swing of a sword, David could have the throne. If David wants it, he can have it. The rationale is obvious. Hasn't God delivered David? Isn't this God's doing? Hasn't God just set up the divine opportunity to take up the spear and finish off Saul? David's counselors certainly think so.

> So David and Abishai came to the people by night; and there Saul lay sleeping within the camp, with his spear stuck in the ground by his head. And Abner and the people lay all around him. Then Abishai said to David, "God has delivered your enemy into your hand this day. Now therefore, please, let me strike him at once with the spear, right to the earth; and I will not have to strike him a second time!"
> **1 Samuel 26:7-8**

Ah, the spear of Saul, waiting there, stuck in the ground, the shaft just waiting for David's hand, only a few inches away! This is surely God's timing. All the running can end tonight. No longer an outlaw. After all, Samuel had already anointed him to be king, years before. This must be the hour; this must be the moment. From the wilderness to the palace with just one thrust of the spear. What a divine opportunity!

God or Spear?

A divine opportunity? No, it's a test from God. Who or what will be David's refuge? Saul's refuge is his spear. For David, the question that night was: Will he join the order of Saul and make the spear his refuge, too? Or will he trust God for the crown—letting God's timing and God's heart open the door? Who or what? God or spear? David replied,

> The Lord forbid that I should stretch out my hand against the Lord's anointed. But please, take now the spear and the jug of water that are by his head, and let us go.
> **1 Samuel 26:11**

David had never learned the manly art of spear-throwing, and he chose not to learn it that night. In fact, he never learned it. Even when he became king.

Fifteen stories are told of David in the wilderness: Two of them reveal the opportunities he had to take out Saul. They are stories of vulnerability and seeming open doors from God to finish off this mad king. Another time, Saul was relieving himself in the cave where David was hiding (1 Samuel 24), and David spared his life. But why?

This is the little detail of our story that catches our attention—David calls Saul "the Lord's anointed." Eugene Peterson writes,

> In the wilderness years, as David was dealing with God, a sense of the sacred developed in him. While he was living in that austere country, his awareness of holiness, of God's beauty and presence in everything, in everyone, increased exponentially.[92]

The wilderness, the rejection, the austerity was teaching David a new kind of trust, a new way of beauty, a new depth of refuge. As David hid in caves, he found the beauty of the darkness and the protection of the cool wet walls as a reminder to him of God's protection and love. The holiness of the wilderness was the refuge he was finding in God. David had deepened in his view of God's anointing, and God's anointed.

Saul was God's anointed? David could see God's calling upon Saul, and he was not going to violate what God had anointed. David was not going to be a practiced and refined spear-thrower. Rather, he had learned the lesson of the wilderness—*I will make You my refuge, and as such, I will wait on You O Lord. I will trust Your timing for the work you have for me to do.*[93]

For many men, especially most leaders, and many, many pastors, spear-throwing is an art form. Whether it's responding to the way our wives speak to us at home, how we speak of the competition at work, or in the case of the Church, who out there is teaching "heresy," we learn very easily how to sling the spear.

David never learned the art and, it appears from Scripture, never cared to. David's refuge was not primarily in combating evil but in cultivating love. In the wilderness David found God, his soul discovered the mercy of God, and his heart was broken through the pain he endured. In the psalm he wrote just after the cave incident with Saul, we can feel the heart of a man who is growing into a worshipper and warrior.

> *Be merciful to me, O God, be merciful to me! For my soul trusts in You;*
> *And in the shadow of Your wings I will make my refuge,*
> *Until these calamities have passed by.*
>
> *I will cry out to God Most High,*
> *To God who performs all things for me.*
>
> *He shall send from heaven and save me;*
> *He reproaches the one who would swallow me up. Selah*
> *God shall send forth His mercy and His truth.*
> **Psalm 57:1-3**

All over the Psalms, we find this word, *refuge*, thirty-seven times. The wilderness was the dictionary and Saul the thesaurus for David learning the meaning and purpose of this word. David was being transformed from a potential spear-thrower to a powerful mercy-seeker. This is the mercy David exhibits toward Saul.

A refuge is vital in the wilderness. Once, while hiking with my father on the Appalachian trail, we were suddenly engulfed in a blinding rain storm. According to our map, we were closing in on a lean-to, a wooden A-frame constructed of two-by-fours in the woods along the trail. We ran through the storm, found the dilapidated structure (probably built in the 1930s by the Roosevelt Conservation Corps). But we didn't care about that—it was dry and safe. We had found a refuge.

Messy Living

David learned of God as refuge in such a setting—the wilderness. David's prayer for God to be his refuge was a cry of distress that brought comfort. It is most often through distress that we discover the glory of God. He continues in his Psalm,

> *My soul is among lions; I lie among the sons of men*
> *Who are set on fire,*
> *Whose teeth are spears and arrows,*
> *And their tongue a sharp sword.*
>
> *Be exalted, O God, above the heavens;*
> *Let Your glory be above all the earth.*
> **Psalm 57:4-5**

Ironically it was in running for his life that David found life: He discovered God as his refuge. One of the surprises of spirituality is that it's in our messiness that God brings order. Our outer life becomes a mess, so our inner life can be brought to order. This is what makes David the forerunner of wholehearted living—the Books of Samuel show us the mess of his outer life, and the Psalms show us the order of his inner life. But without the messiness, God never would have become David's refuge. Desperation is the beginning of freedom.

The wilderness and the stressors of life mean nothing until they drive us to God. The great missionary J. Hudson Taylor once said, "It's not the pressure that matters but what you do with the pressure. Either it pushes you away from God or presses you into God." Most of us miss the point and fight the process. David became a spear target but never a spear-thrower. David had to learn to press into God.

Another One who came a thousand years later never took up the spear but was thrust through by one: Jesus. He said, "love your enemies" and "pray for those who spitefully use you," and He lived it. He was stripped, beaten, and cut by the spear. He then asked God to forgive. David is the forerunner of a new order, the order of love, the order of refuge. Jesus fulfilled it. David and Jesus show us how it works in the real world.

Saul runs after David; David runs to God. The Jews chase Jesus; Jesus chases His Father. David found God to be His refuge, and Jesus surrendered His spirit on the cross to His Lord. So it is for us. Who is throwing spears at you? Who is running after you? Who are you running to? We are going to face spear-throwers and sword-wielders, but instead of pulling out our own, God calls us to trust in Him.

The wilderness is a dangerous place. There are dangerous people out there whom we certainly shouldn't trust, but God uses the wilderness and wild people to cause us to find our heart's refuge in Him. Run to God. Run to Christ. He promises to be your refuge.

The Dangerous Excursion: Day 13

1. Who is casting spears at you right now? How are you responding?

2. From reading Psalm 57, how does David make God his refuge?

3. How can you make God your refuge? What do you need to do?

DAY 14: INTIMACY

1 Samuel 30

1 Now it happened, when David and his men came to Ziklag, on the third day, that the Amalekites had invaded the South and Ziklag, attacked Ziklag and burned it with fire, 2 and had taken captive the women and those who were there, from small to great; they did not kill anyone, but carried them away and went their way. 3 So David and his men came to the city, and there it was, burned with fire; and their wives, their sons, and their daughters had been taken captive. 4 Then David and the people who were with him lifted up their voices and wept, until they had no more power to weep. 5 And David's two wives, Ahinoam the Jezreelitess, and Abigail the widow of Nabal the Carmelite, had been taken captive. 6 Now David was greatly distressed, for the people spoke of stoning him, because the soul of all the people was grieved, every man for his sons and his daughters. But David strengthened himself in the Lord his God.

7 Then David said to Abiathar the priest, Ahimelech's son, "Please bring the ephod here to me." And Abiathar brought the ephod to David. 8 So David inquired of the Lord, saying, "Shall I pursue this troop? Shall I overtake them?" And He answered him, "Pursue, for you shall surely overtake them and without fail recover all."

9 So David went, he and the six hundred men who were with him, and came to the Brook Besor, where those stayed who were left behind. 10 But David pursued, he and four hundred men; for two hundred stayed behind, who were so weary that they could not cross the Brook Besor ...

17 Then David attacked them from twilight until the evening of the next day. Not a man of them escaped, except four hundred young men who rode on camels and fled. 18 So David recovered all that the Amalekites had carried away, and David rescued his two wives. 19 And nothing of theirs was lacking, either small or great, sons or daughters, spoil or anything which they had taken from them; David recovered all. 20 Then David took all the flocks and herds they had driven before those other livestock, and said, "This is David's spoil."

Gary Larson was a cartoonist made famous for his syndicated strip *The Far Side*. In one cartoon, two deer are in the woods; one has a bullseye on his front shoulder. The other deer is looking at it and observes, "Bummer of a birthmark, Hal." This just might be the way to describe David at this time in his life. Everywhere he turns, someone wants him dead.

How would you like to go from being the rising star of Israel to the Mossad's Top 10 Most Wanted? That's David's life now.

This just might be lowest of the low points in David's heart. It's as if his life has become one continuous wanted poster across the land. In the late nineteenth century, people said the notorious bank and train robbers Butch Cassidy and the Sundance Kid were so notorious that they had to leave the country. Even in the vast West, they had no place to hide. As the famous Pinkerton Investigation Company began to hunt them down, the only place they knew to go was Argentina. The Pinkerton investigators told the Argentine police, so the duo ran to Bolivia, where they perished in a final gunfight. David would have understood their plight.

Compromise

In fleeing for his life, David leaves Saul's Israel and escapes into Philistine-controlled towns and cities. He now dwells in the occupied zone of the Philistines (1 Samuel 27-30). Achish, the king of the Philistines, has given David a city to dwell in, Ziklag. This is a trying and difficult time in David's life. Out of desperation, he has befriended his enemies and for the past year has had some semblance of normalcy for his family and the families of his men. He has compromised his trust in God, and the result is a mess as great as anything he has faced with Saul.

While on a mission for the Philistines, David leaves his family and those of his men unprotected. Another enemy—a new one for David—takes advantage of the situation and attacks.

Now it happened, when David and his men came to Ziklag, on the third day, that the Amalekites had invaded the South and Ziklag, attacked Ziklag and burned it with fire, and had taken captive the women and those who were there, from small to great; they did not kill anyone, but carried them away and went their way. So David and his men came to the city, and there it was, burned with fire; and their wives, their sons, and their daughters had been taken captive.
1 Samuel 30:1-3

Compromise always leads to a new set of problems and enemies. David's men are in a city they shouldn't be in, befriended by people they shouldn't trust, and now have a situation they can't navigate. But matters are about to get worse.

Then David and the people who were with him lifted up their voices and wept, until they had no more power to weep. And David's two wives, Ahinoam the Jezreelitess, and Abigail the widow of Nabal the Carmelite, had been taken captive. Now David was greatly distressed, for the people spoke of stoning him, because the soul of all the people was grieved, every man for his sons and his daughters.
1 Samuel 30: 4-6

I believe this is the greatest test of David's life. Not only is David distressed over his predicament from the Amalekites, he is also in danger of losing the trust of his men. He's about to lose everything!

What David does next will determine his destiny. How David handles his own compromised position will pave the way for his future.

Too many of us panic in such times. Too many of us compromise from our last compromise. Compromise always leads to more compromise. When we start learning the way of compromise, it's never ending. We take the way of least resistance and miss God's best.

What does David do? He could have called a board meeting. He could have reasoned with his men. He could have called for a vote. He could have just given up. Who would have blamed him? Desperate times call for a reasonable response, right? Not necessarily. David makes a choice he has learned in the wilderness—the way of the road less traveled.

David turns to God.

The great "but" of the Bible. I love the "buts" of the Bible. Often the "buts" of the Bible are the doors to miracles. Look what David does next. It's amazing and courageous!

> But David strengthened himself in the Lord his God.
> *I Samuel 30: 6*

David cries out. He's not going to trust anyone but God! Take a moment and ponder these words: But David strengthened himself in the Lord his God. Is there any more profound sentence in all the Bible? Is there any other place in the chronicles of David that more defines him as a worshipper and warrior?

Engagement with God

I hesitate to define worship, for there are so many definitions, but I will venture to say one of the best is *engagement with God*. Worship is intimacy, and intimacy is engagement with God. It is living a life with people but not *for* people. It's having a job with work to be done, but it's not living *for* the work. It is living, working, and having our being *in* God, for an audience of One. Mike Pilavachi describes it as "living a devoted life in His presence. Worship is about God, to God, and for God."[94] David is choosing to engage with God before he engages with men.

The audience for whom David is most concerned is not his army of men, but God. He has no one else who can love him, forgive him, bless him, and instruct him; just God. He has grown to understand that simple but profound truth—trust God. David has learned trust in the wilderness, in caves, under trees, and in the hills around Bethlehem. Now more than ever, his trust is tested, and his gut reaction is to engage the Lord.

What about you? This life is not a dress rehearsal for someday meeting Jesus face to face. This life is preparation for that day through knowing Christ right now. This life, with all its pain, disappointments, and hurts, is ushering in the experience of intimacy with Jesus that will culminate in actually gazing into His eyes of love. This intimacy begins now and can be experienced in the give-and-take of hardship on this earth today.

David is actualizing the encounter of intimacy by remaining in Him. With all his circumstances crashing in around him, David is choosing obedience by staying connected to the heart of his Lord. David wants to know God's heart. Jesus, in describing the experience of intimacy, likens our love relationship with God to that of a vine in vineyard.

> *"I am the Vine, you are the branches. When you're joined with me and I with you, the relation intimate and organic, the harvest is sure to be abundant. Separated, you can't produce a thing. Anyone who separates from me is deadwood, gathered up and thrown on the bonfire. But if you make yourselves at home with me and my words are at home in you, you can be sure that whatever you ask will be listened to and acted upon. This is how my Father shows who he is— when you produce grapes, when you mature as my disciples.*
>
> *"I've loved you the way my Father has loved me. Make yourselves at home in my love. If you keep my commands, you'll remain intimately at home in my love. That's what I've done—kept my Father's commands and made myself at home in his love.*
> **John 15 – MSG**

David is retreating to the only home he has. He has no home in Israel. He has no home in the Philistine-occupied zone. He may not even have a family at this point. But David knows he has an intimate home in the heart of God. It's a home no one can steal, and no army can conquer.

The Sanctuary

I have a pastor friend who lost his job in a prominent church. He not only lost his church; he lost his wife, too. She filed for divorce and soon remarried. Being a pastor and a father was all this man had ever known. In a matter of just a couple of years, he lost everything that he held important and valuable. He had a glimpse of himself as a loser and a failure. In desperation, he took to the road and drove to California, his childhood home. It was there, looking out on the ocean from the high cliffs of southern California, that he began to glimpse God in a new way.

He found the sanctuary of God and began to rebuild his life. Brennan Manning explains,

> Spirituality is not one compartment or sphere of life. Rather it is a lifestyle: the process of life lived with a vision of faith. Sanctity lies in discovering my true self, moving toward it, and living out of it.[95]

Sanctuary is defined as "a sacred place." For many of us the word itself seems to conjure up pictures of cathedrals, monasteries, and holy places. But sanctuary, as I define it, is less of a place and more of a relationship, a lifestyle. It is a sacred encounter with God. Sanctuary is whenever and wherever we meet God and God meets us. Intimacy with God is the sanctuary where we find Him. It's that place of actual love and acceptance where God meets us and loves us.

The sanctuary of intimacy is the place in our daily work where we commune and abide in Christ. It's daily and it's a learned behavior. The sanctuary of God is the moment we choose to abide in Christ and let Christ abide in us. In this direction of our heart, intimacy is formed.

When our heart becomes the heart of God, we have a sanctuary where our cries for help are heard and our agonies are most deeply understood. The sanctuary of God becomes the home of our heart. It's a home of love and intimacy. The sacred place of communing with God pulls us out of the world of deadlines, bottom lines, and harassing employees. It is that place of sacred peace and sacred focus. It's the place of honesty and intimacy.

Waiting on God

In Psalm 25, David captures the sanctuary of his heart. In this poem we recognize not only the utter impossibility of his situation, but the union he has with God,

> *To You, O Lord, I lift up my soul.*
> *O my God, I trust in You;*
> *Let me not be ashamed;*
> *Let not my enemies triumph over me.*
>
> *Indeed, let no one who waits on You be ashamed;*
> *Let those be ashamed who deal treacherously without cause.*

WORSHIPPER WARRIOR

Show me Your ways, O Lord;
Teach me Your paths.
Lead me in Your truth, and teach me ...
On You I wait all the day.

Remember, O Lord, Your tender mercies and Your
lovingkindnesses.
Psalm 25: 1-6

David lifts his heart up to God in a time of trouble. He is desperate. He must hear from God! He begins this poem with a declaration that come what may, he is going to trust in God. He is aware that he just might lose everything. His enemies want to triumph and shame him. David, in lifting his soul to the Lord, exclaims that he will wait on the Lord for as long as it takes to know God's path. This is the cry of a son to His loving Father— a heavenly Father whom he views as full of tender mercies and full of lovingkindness. Intimacy.

Cultivating an intimacy that can wait on God in prayer is one of the most vital and dynamic disciplines in the life of a worshipper and warrior. The word "wait" means to "bind together through a process of intertwining." Waiting on God is a cultivation of an intimate relationship of being in the presence of God and listening for His promptings.

Waiting in prayer is just as much about becoming something as getting something. It is often overlooked in our understanding of prayer that when we pray and wait on God for an answer, God is changing us from the inside out through the very process of waiting. Waiting is an active verb! This waiting on God is the journey of braiding God's heart into ours through seeking, crying out, and listening. As we seek the Lord, we come into a deepening knowledge of His heart, His ways, and His paths. Our wills are transformed through our active seeking.

This weaving of our will into God's will through an intimate, vital, dynamic relationship is the very essence of being a worshipper and warrior. Eugene Peterson captures the essence of this in his paraphrase of Jesus' admonition in how to pray,

Our Father in heaven,
Reveal who you are.
Matthew 6:9 MSG

Prayer reveals Who God is and who we aren't. It is as we seek the Lord in prayer that He weaves His heart into ours.

Are you in a place in your life where you need to hear from God? Are you in a time of desperation, anxiety, or just needing wisdom from God? Don't miss the deeper truth that as you seek the Lord, He is knitting your heart to His. As you seek the Lord for an answer, He is transforming you. Intimacy with Jesus is the goal; transformation is the result.

The Dangerous Excursion: Day 14

1. **How would you define intimacy with the Lord?**

2. **What in your life is God is prompting you to seek Him about?**

3. **How is the Lord weaving His heart into yours in this journey of seeking?**

DAY 15: CONDITIONS

Psalm 144
1 Blessed be the Lord my Rock,
  Who trains my hands for war,
  And my fingers for battle—
  2 My lovingkindness and my fortress,
  My high tower and my deliverer,
  My shield and the One in whom I take refuge,
  Who subdues my people under me.
3 Lord, what is man, that You take knowledge of him?
  Or the son of man, that You are mindful of him?
  4 Man is like a breath;
  His days are like a passing shadow.
5 Bow down Your heavens, O Lord, and come down;
  Touch the mountains, and they shall smoke.
  6 Flash forth lightning and scatter them;
  Shoot out Your arrows and destroy them.
  7 Stretch out Your hand from above;
  Rescue me and deliver me out of great waters,
  From the hand of foreigners,
  8 Whose mouth speaks lying words,
  And whose right hand is a right hand of falsehood.
9 I will sing a new song to You, O God;
  On a harp of ten strings I will sing praises to You,
  10 The One who gives salvation to kings,
  Who delivers David His servant
  From the deadly sword.
11 Rescue me and deliver me from the hand of foreigners,
  Whose mouth speaks lying words,
  And whose right hand is a right hand of falsehood—
  12 That our sons may be as plants grown up in their youth;
  That our daughters may be as pillars,
  Sculptured in palace style;
  13 That our barns may be full,
  Supplying all kinds of produce;

That our sheep may bring forth thousands
And ten thousands in our fields;
14 That our oxen may be well laden;
That there be no breaking in or going out;
That there be no outcry in our streets.
15 Happy are the people who are in such a state;
Happy are the people whose God is the Lord!

David never completely withdraws from society to be alone with God. He is no monk or desert priest who lives his life in obscurity in order to find God. He is in the wilderness, but he is not retreating there to escape the realities of life or the pressures of leadership. David is in the wilderness because that is the condition of his life.

David rarely speaks of being with the Lord in quiet just for the sake of being alone with God. David's life is energetic, active, and aggressive. David's life is his work, and his work is what he speaks about the most. David is an at-work warrior who works from the vantage point of worship.

When we look at the actual work David does, we may be shocked. Eugene Peterson says, "David's primary work is war. Most of the work that David exults in doing because God makes it possible for him to do it has to do with killing people. His work world features weapons and fighting."[96] We cannot understand the robust life of David without understanding his conditions.

Our lives are not like David's in the literal sense of fighting bloody battles. But I believe life is a connection of battles fought relationally and at work. Have you ever looked at life as a string of battles? Through the early years of childhood to our first job, marriage, job changes, and friendships, we can see a life of warfare, of bad and good decisions, of failures and victories. Psalm 144 is a poem for the battle-experienced man!

Fusion

We cannot grasp the heart of David—his prayers, his poems, his friendships, his sufferings—without understanding the context of his work conditions. It is through them that David prays and worships. In writing his poetry, he is making something with words that describe his world. Prayer and the conditions of his life go hand-in-hand.

The poem of Psalm 144 is the fusion in words of David's past and present life conditions. God's past actions never remain in the past but are lifted into the present by his prayers. David is exalting the Lord from his past experience with Him. He extols all that God has done in the past, even as it forges his heart for the future. David's view of God begins with the experiential knowledge of his deliverance and his expectation of how God will show up again in his present conditions.

> *Blessed be the Lord my Rock,*
> *Who trains my hands for war,*
> *And my fingers for battle.*
> **Psalm 144: 1**

David's story is one of surrender—not on the battlefield, but within his heart. What David could never do for himself, God does. David understands the Lord as the One who has trained him for the work he has been called to do. God has equipped David's heart for the work set before him. I have often called Psalm 144 the "Anthem of the Worshipper and Warrior" because no other poem so encapsulates the heart of the man who passionately wants God under the most strenuous and challenging of life's circumstances.

David is infused with energy through the power of God in his life. He believes the Lord is truly the One who has made him into a warrior. From shepherd to warrior prince in just a few short years, God's behind it. God's leading it.

Don't miss this: Our lives as Jesus' disciples is never devoid of our conditions. Most of us look at our birthplace, our race, our parents, and our jobs, as only assumptions. We look at our conditions and absorb them into our daily life. Yet none of this happens in a vacuum. God is forming you through conditions.

David is born into conditions of Philistine power, the birth of the Iron

Age, with violence and sex pervading everything in Palestine. David is not exempt from its influence on his life. He is rather a product of his conditions. And so are we. Our conditions, favorable and unfavorable, are the life into which we are born.

Baptized for Conditions

The twenty-first century is not altogether different from the conditions David faced. We are surrounded by pervasive violence and promiscuous sex. We wake up daily to another terrorist attack, another sensual ad on the right-hand column of our favorite news app. Not much has changed. This is the human condition, and it's here that holy living must work.

God doesn't baptize our conditions, He baptizes *us*! The God who birthed you and me into these conditions is the same God who birthed David into his. Most of his conditions were unfavorable, and so are ours. But David makes an anthem to the battle of life through his poem.

God desires to be our Rock—the Foundation of our living. And as our Foundation, He longs to train us for war under highly unfavorable conditions. He wants to train you and me to war for His cause upon the earth. But He cannot train and equip us without being first and foremost our Rock, our solid unchanging Cornerstone. More than anyone else, the Apostle Paul captured the meaning of this metaphor.

> *Now, therefore, you are no longer strangers and foreigners, but fellow citizens with the saints and members of the household of God, having been built on the foundation of the apostles and prophets, Jesus Christ Himself being the chief cornerstone, in whom the whole building, being fitted together, grows into a holy temple in the Lord, in whom you also are being built together for a dwelling place of God in the Spirit.*
> **Ephesians 2:19-22**

We are being built together with other men of God, with other bloodstained allies, into the dwelling place of intimacy with Jesus. Intimacy trains our hands for battle. Intimacy draws us into the place of becoming a holy temple of God, a place where the Spirit can dwell and empower us for the conditions of our lives.

My lovingkindness and my fortress,
My high tower and my deliverer,
My shield and the One in whom I take refuge,
Who subdues my people under me.
Psalm 144:2

David now stacks up earthy metaphors of God being his fortress, tower, deliverer, shield, and refuge under the rubric of lovingkindness. It is the lovingness of God, the kindness of God (literally what it means in Hebrew) pulled together poetically to emphasize why He is a fortress, tower, and deliverer. These are the conditions of David's personal experience with God.

The lovingkindness of God is our fortress, our high tower, our deliverer, our shield, and our refuge. God is not separate from His attributes. We discover the heart of God most deeply through His lovingkindness. It is in our belovedness that we come to experience the safety of God's heart. It is only as we experience God's love in our conditions that we truly discover His heart. Under a life of unfavorable conditions—attacks at our job, marriage struggles, and the war of relationships—we become men who are trained for battle. God's lovingkindness is the place to which we must retreat. It is the place of our greatest strength.

Stretch out Your hand from above;
Rescue me and deliver me out of great waters,
From the hand of foreigners,

Whose mouth speaks lying words,
And whose right hand is a right hand of falsehood.
Psalm 144:7-8

Who better than David to speak of deception and betrayal? The right hand of fellowship becomes the right hand of falsehood. From Saul to his own son Absalom, David will know what it feels like to be ripped off. These are the conditions of our lives, and this is the prayer for all of us.

Conditioned to Conqueror

I have a close friend who is being powerfully used by God all over the country as an evangelist. His childhood in Louisiana involved repeated beatings, sexual abuse, and deception. He is who he is because of his past conditions. But God made him a warrior through them. As crappy as they were, those conditions are what God most used in his life to make him a worshipper and warrior who is now reaching some of the most hardened criminals in America. Most recently he has been working with soldiers suffering from post-traumatic stress disorder and the inner demons they are experiencing.

God wants to be our Warrior. God wants to fight and defend us. What greater news is there? This is the way of God Almighty—He will go to battle for us. You are conditioned to be a conqueror because *He* is your Conqueror. In times of deep sorrow, He wants us to cry out for His power to be stretched out upon our condition. The worshipper and warrior is *not* one who takes matters into his own hands but rather calls out to God from the fortress of His lovingkindness—for God to protect us, guide, and live through us!

> *I will sing a new song to You, O God;*
> *On a harp of ten strings I will sing praises to You,*
>
> *The One who gives salvation to kings,*
> *Who delivers David His servant*
> *From the deadly sword.*
> **Psalm 144:10-11**

David learned in the worst of conditions to worship. He sang and prayed his way out of his troubles. David learned the great secret of overcoming—worship, looking up. Often, we think of worship in terms of singing some songs at church. That's about it; no more to it than that. Just sing through some boring songs with lots of repeatable verses that make little sense in our real world of battle and then go home. We do it for our wives. Right? You know it's true. Worship is nothing more than singing old worn-out hymns or seven-eleven songs—seven stanzas repeated eleven times!

But not for David, and not for the true worshipper and warrior. Worship is a lifestyle; it is focus, not so much in how we sing, but rather the direction of our heart. David is singing a new song, a battle song, a warfare poem to the King who has delivered him out of bondage. For David and for us, worship is taking our eyes off our battles and inviting Jesus into them. Yes, inviting Jesus into our war-torn marriage, our war-torn work, our conditions. Conditions drive us to Jesus.

> *Rescue me and deliver me from the hand of foreigners,*
> *Whose mouth speaks lying words,*
> *And whose right hand is a right hand of falsehood—*
>
> *That our sons may be as plants grown up in their youth;*
> *That our daughters may be as pillars,*
> *Sculptured in palace style;*
>
> *That our barns may be full,*
> *Supplying all kinds of produce;*
> *That our sheep may bring forth thousands*
> *And ten thousands in our fields;*
>
> *That our oxen may be well laden;*
> *That there be no breaking in or going out;*
> *That there be no outcry in our streets.*
> **Psalm 144:11-13**

This is the purpose of the warfare. This is the value God places upon our heritage of battles fought. Men, He is molding you into one who overcomes, who fights through the wars of our life. You are called "more than a conqueror." You are created to win in this life. The battles of your conditions are battles that you are now equipped to win.

This is the point of Paul, who had weathered some of the most horrendous storms life could throw any man—separation from his family, torture, shipwreck, beatings, and persecution.

> *Yet in all these things we are more than conquerors through Him*
> *who loved us. For I am persuaded that neither death nor life, nor*
> *angels nor principalities nor powers, nor things present nor things*
> *to come, nor height nor depth, nor any other created thing, shall*
> *be able to separate us from the love of God which is in Christ*
> *Jesus our Lord.*
> **Romans 8: 37-39**

What does it take for you to give up? For David, for Paul, nothing life threw their way was going to stop them. Paul envisions a glorious future and he is unstoppable. David sees a time of blessing coming. He is looking forward to that time of God's outpouring upon his labor.

The Happy Warrior

So, let me repeat my question: What is hindering you from the blessings of God? Satan wants to take you out, drive you out. He will use depression, loss of work, financial ruin, divorce, drugs, you name it. But will you fight for God's blessing? Will you choose to envision a future of reward? David concludes,

> *Happy are the people who are in such a state;*
> *Happy are the people whose God is the Lord!*
> **Psalm 144:15**

Just the other day, a friend called me to share of her betrayal by a missions group many years ago. She and her husband are new to our church, and as I asked some questions she opened up about a condition they encountered in Czechoslovakia. The condition of being betrayed and lied to led them to come back to the United States with no financial backing and few friends. It was horrific, unjust, and difficult.

But the aftermath has brought them into a greater joy and deeper walk with God. They learned to depend on the Holy Spirit like never before. With no funding, no job, and few contacts, they literally had to start over again in their fifties. But they chose to trust God. They came into an intimacy with Jesus and each other that, she admitted to me, could not have occurred without the pain of betrayal. They now have a deep abiding relationship with the Lord and each other as a result.

The Anthem of the Worshipper and Warrior, Psalm 144, concludes with "*Happy are the people in who are in such a state*." Which state? The state of verses 3-8, in the midst of lying words and falsehood? Or the state of verses 9-15? Which is it?

The answer is yes! Yes, all of them. David wrote the poem because of pain and hardship; and his conclusions? That victory can come through deep conditions of lies and betrayal! Yes, that is "the happy state."

Conditions are God's field of maturity. Conditions are God's training center to build a man. You and I are being forged through battle. Our heart can be happy and joyful if, and—don't miss this, only if—God is becoming our Lord through our conditions. Don't quit; battle! Battle in worship, prayer, and obedience.

The Dangerous Excursion: Day 15

1. What part of Psalm 144 do you relate to the most and why?

2. What about your current conditions are difficult and painful?

3. As a result of this chapter, what are you going to do differently in your life when difficult hardships come your way?

DAY 16: IDENTITY

Psalm 27
1 The Lord is my light and my salvation;
   Whom shall I fear?
   The Lord is the strength of my life;
   Of whom shall I be afraid?
   2 When the wicked came against me
   To eat up my flesh,
   My enemies and foes,
   They stumbled and fell.
   3 Though an army may encamp against me,
   My heart shall not fear;
   Though war may rise against me,
   In this I will be confident.

4 One thing I have desired of the Lord,
   That will I seek:
   That I may dwell in the house of the Lord
   All the days of my life,
   To behold the beauty of the Lord,
   And to inquire in His temple.
   5 For in the time of trouble
   He shall hide me in His pavilion;
   In the secret place of His tabernacle
   He shall hide me;
   He shall set me high upon a rock.

6 And now my head shall be lifted up above my enemies all around me;
   Therefore I will offer sacrifices of joy in His tabernacle;
   I will sing, yes, I will sing praises to the Lord.
7 Hear, O Lord, when I cry with my voice!
   Have mercy also upon me, and answer me.
   8 When You said, "Seek My face,"
   My heart said to You, "Your face, Lord, I will seek."
   9 Do not hide Your face from me;

Do not turn Your servant away in anger;
You have been my help;
Do not leave me nor forsake me,
O God of my salvation.
10 When my father and my mother forsake me,
Then the Lord will take care of me.

11 Teach me Your way, O Lord,
And lead me in a smooth path, because of my enemies.
12 Do not deliver me to the will of my adversaries;
For false witnesses have risen against me,
And such as breathe out violence.
13 I would have lost heart, unless I had believed
That I would see the goodness of the Lord
In the land of the living.

14 Wait on the Lord;
Be of good courage,
And He shall strengthen your heart;
Wait, I say, on the Lord!

At this point we have read enough into 1 Samuel and the Psalms to not only begin to form an impression of David the man, but to also observe the contrast between his life and Saul's. The difference between the two men is a lesson in identity.

Saul has now been king, the CEO of Israel, for over seventeen years. His life is a story of unprecedented opportunity, frenzied speed, and impetuous decisions. He has lived a reality show of wealth, power, and prestige. He is The Man. Everyone in Israel follows his every tweet. Yet, from God's perspective, he has made one disastrous decision after another. Something is wrong in Saul's heart. As a poser before the prophet Samuel, he has been found out. As a pretender before his son Jonathan, even he can feel the loss of respect.

One moment he is the supposed worshipper of God and the next he is overwhelmed with jealousy and murderous rage. His is a life of the religious fake, the sycophant, who is two-faced and lives in a half-hearted world of falsehood. He's fooling no one but himself. Jesus called such men hypocrites. I would call him a phony and poser.

A Radical Paradigm

But David, with none of the benefits of Saul—no position of power, no home, no prestige, and a reputation before men as an outlaw—has never lost his core identity. Through all the bloodshed and betrayals, the battles and disappointments, David has stayed true to his heart for God. The very first description given of him, at the beginning of our journey into his life, is that he is a man after God's own heart. What the Lord sought for, way back seventeen years before, hasn't changed: "The Lord has sought for Himself a man after His own heart, and the Lord has commanded him to be commander over His people."[97]

David's paradigm for life is being loved by God. David's core identity is a heart-to-heart love relationship with God. His life is a radical pursuit of God's heart. Even with the disastrous choices and the magnificent mistakes he will make (coming up in our last chapters), the Bible still describes David as a man who related to, identified with, and pursued the love of God, the heart of God. David's core identity was in being beloved. David's core reality was his intimate relationship with God. We observe David in all his authenticity in this beautiful poem:

> *The Lord is my light and my salvation;*
> *Whom shall I fear?*
> *The Lord is the strength of my life;*
> *Of whom shall I be afraid?*
>
> *When the wicked came against me*
> *To eat up my flesh,*
> *My enemies and foes,*
> *They stumbled and fell.*
>
> *Though an army may encamp against me,*
> *My heart shall not fear;*
> *Though war may rise against me,*
> *In this I will be confident.*
> ***Psalm 27: 1-3***

For Saul, for most men, our identity is formed by our outward accomplishments and achievements. Our identity is the way we define ourselves or how we measure what we define as success or failure. This is one of, if not the most, important issues of life—how we define our identity. We have been taught since our childhood to define success in light of our work, our position, and our paycheck. As a pastor and counselor, I spend hours each week listening to the battles of men's lives. Rarely do I meet a man who has found a definition of his identity in anything less than how he is scoring on the success track of his job, his marriage, or his 401k. Thus, his life is as unpredictable as springtime in the Rockies. One day he's up and the next day's he's down. One day is sunshine and the next a blizzard.

Measures of Success

Our identity could be defined as how we measure our value in life. Our value is interwoven into a view of who we are and how we define success. For all of us men, this is complicated; most of us mirror the values of our parents and upbringing. Even for most Christians, the measurement of our value, our identity, is taken from our culture. If we are a successful CEO we are valuable. If we are overlooked for that promotion, we are not.

If you were to ask any man who has just been fired or gone through a divorce what his life means, he would say it's in tatters. His security is shattered and his identity is in question. I counseled a man in our church recently who just lost his job of twenty-five years, and he was confused and questioned everything. He was close to jettisoning all faith in God.

We all have wounded hearts and battered selves. What do we do when we fully realize that our identity is wrapped up in all things outward? Maybe, just maybe, that's the beginning of healing. Brennan Manning writes, "The Spiritual life begins with the acceptance of our wounded self." [98] But there's the rub: It's in the wounded self, the misplaced identity.

David's view of his life is radically different than ours. David's identity is found in his experience of God's love and the intimacy of God's heart. The fourteenth-century mystic Julian of Norwich might have been describing David when he said, "Our courteous Lord does not want his servants to despair because they fall often and grievously; for our falling does not hinder him in loving us." [99] David, even in his despair, found meaning through his experience of God's love.

God loves the man he created; God loves who we really are—the one who can know and feel love. God loves that little child within that ran to his mother or father for comfort when he fell down and broke out in tears. God loves our heart, the good heart, the transformed heart.

God's love is not conditional but relational.

Yet many of us as men feel so darn inadequate. We are convinced that we don't have what it takes. We loathe the man we have become, and we hate the way we act. We know that phony side of our religious posturing. This comes out in our self-talk as we recite the script we heard growing up: "You're such a loser," "You'll never be successful," and such accusations as "What kind of a man would do *that*?" Self-hatred and the broodings of our self-diagnosed identity cripple us from experiencing God's love. Henri Nouwen has said,

> Over the years I have come to realize that the greatest trap in our life is not success, popularity, and power but self-rejection … When we have come to believe the voices that call us worthless and unlovable, then success, popularity, and power are easily perceived as attractive solutions.[100]

For me, it was losing my position at the church I had built. For the colonel I counseled last month, it was the shock of being overlooked for a key leadership position at the Air Force Academy. It is in such times of perceived rejection that we ask the deeper questions of identity: *Who am I? What is my worth? Why am I important?*

David's focus, David's identity, is a radical paradigm of love from and for God. He knows he's loved by God, and it is this very passion that gets God's attention and sets him apart. God notices David because David takes notice of God! *"The Lord has sought for Himself a man after His own heart."* God sees David's heart because David is gazing at His heart. David's security is in his intimacy with God.

Beloved of God

David would write, "The Lord is my shepherd, I shall not want" (Psalm 23:1). "*As the deer pants for the water brooks, so pants my heart for You, O Lord*" (Psalm 42:1). David defined himself as radically beloved of God! He had made the Lord and His immense love for him the measure of his personal worth. God's love for him, God's choosing him, was the paradigm David used to define his value. David knows that he is loved, beloved of the Lord!

But we suffer through our lives with an identity based in achievements and the adulation of others.[101] Henri Nouwen, in trying to describe the meaning of life to an agnostic Jewish friend, says it this way: "All I want you to know is that you are beloved ... My only desire is to make these words reverberate in every corner of your being—you are beloved."[102] For most of us, our intrinsic value is based on our success and fulfilling those big dreams. It's a dream of value, of personal worth. And it's a fantasy.

The darkness of our heart defines us. For most of us, as honor increases, we are tempted toward pride and arrogance. When dishonor comes our way, we move toward bitterness and sadness. We are as tossed around in our emotions as the waves of the sea. Our hearts are a thermometer of our outward dealings with the world. We become spiritual schizophrenics with no deep anchors in our heart.

Now don't get me wrong: I'm not saying our work is unimportant or that we are all called to live as monks, dedicating every ounce of our energy to singing Gregorian chants. Not at all. As I mentioned on Day Six, God has given each of us assignments—work that we are called to do. We are given the mandate in Genesis 1 to "be fruitful and multiply." But our identity is deeper than just what we do. What we *do* with our life is secondary. Our primary identity is experiencing the love of God. Brennan Manning captured the essence of our true identity when he wrote,

> God created us for union with himself: This is the original purpose of our lives. And God is defined as love (1 John 4:16). Living in awareness of our belovedness is the axis around which the

Christian life revolves. Being the beloved is our identity, the core of our existence. It is not merely a lofty thought, an inspiring idea, or one name among many. It is the name by which God knows us and the way he relates to us.[103]

Who am I? I am one loved by God. What is success? It's experiencing God's love! David knows this. David defines his identity by writing,

One thing I have desired of the Lord,
That will I seek:
That I may dwell in the house of the Lord
All the days of my life,
To behold the beauty of the Lord,
And to inquire in His temple.

For in the time of trouble
He shall hide me in His pavilion;
In the secret place of His tabernacle
He shall hide me;
He shall set me high upon a rock.
Psalm 27: 4-5

David's one thing is a growing heart-to-heart, intimate relationship with God! This is David's measure of success. The relentless love of God can rewrite the script of your identity. You are beloved of God—no matter how unsuccessful you are, no matter how successful you are—God's passionate love never changes. Jesus desires to give you a radically new paradigm for defining success.

Who are you? You are one loved by God. "For God so loved *you*" (my emphasis) is another way to read the famous passage from John 3:16. Your identity rests in the persistent, unabating love of God toward you. That's who you are. That's the core identity of a worshipper and warrior.

Waste Your Life

This is radical stuff! To discover our identity in being loved by God is no easy task. Our entire paradigm of success is defined with a completely different set of criteria. All it takes is a business party or a church gathering to understand (both are about the same as for as far as conversational content among men): *How's your job? What's happening at work? What are you and Suzie doing for the holidays?* No one's asking about your heart. No one cares really about our intimacy with Jesus.

To pursue our belovedness is a lonely journey, a road less traveled. It takes a radical commitment to seeking God. Such a life of love can only be experienced through a commitment on our part to time alone with God. For David, it was defined upon the hills of Bethlehem as a shepherd; for us it is pulling away daily to seek God's heart. It's that one thing that God noticed in David and Jesus noticed in Mary.

> *As they continued their travel, Jesus entered a village. A woman by the name of Martha welcomed him and made him feel quite at home. She had a sister, Mary, who sat before the Master, hanging on every word he said. But Martha was pulled away by all she had to do in the kitchen. Later, she stepped in, interrupting them. "Master, don't you care that my sister has abandoned the kitchen to me? Tell her to lend me a hand."*
>
> *The Master said, "Martha, dear Martha, you're fussing far too much and getting yourself worked up over nothing. One thing only is essential, and Mary has chosen it—it's the main course, and won't be taken from her."*
> **Luke 10: 38-42 MSG**

Martha is the twenty-first-century Christian! Doing stuff for Jesus. Martha's life was a busy mess of activity that, it seems apparent in our passage, Jesus didn't even care about. Notice that Martha had to interrupt Mary and Jesus just to be noticed by them. Jesus was focused on Mary because she was hanging on every word he said. Jesus wasn't even aware of Martha's frenzied life. Jesus says, "the one thing only," the essential thing, is what Mary had chosen—to hang onto Jesus, to hang onto His words. But what a waste of time!

What a waste. Come on, get real. Who's got time to wait on anything, much less God? I can't even wait in line at the supermarket without getting antsy.

But the way of the heart, the way of new love, is in silence and seeking. Tranquility is what Mary had, and solitude is what you need. Our soul has to make time to settle, to be quiet, to listen. Seeking God, being alone with the Lord, prayer walks, reading God's Word, may all seem to be a waste of precious time. David writes,

> *Truly my soul silently waits for God;*
> *From Him comes my salvation.*
> *He only is my rock and my salvation;*
> *He is my defense;*
> *I shall not be greatly moved.*
> **Psalm 62: 1-2**

We just cannot discover our belovedness without hearing God's voice. We cannot hear God's voice without listening to Him. This takes time; this takes effort.

Right now as I write, I'm at one of my favorite spots in the world, a cabin in the Rocky Mountains that I have named the Agape Cabin. I come here periodically to escape the frenzy of church work, appointments, and pressure. I'm here alone with my Bible, journal, and laptop. I can hear Canadian geese squawking on the frozen lake nearby and a distant eagle circling overhead. Early this morning, I went on a hike along a rocky crag. I came to listen.

I need such times. I need to find my heart. It seems that church life, busyness, the American dream, works to control our hearts. Every night the news gets worse and the dreams we work so hard to accomplish turn into fleeting vapors. It's no different today than thousands of years ago. As you have now read for the past two weeks, David's life is an endless barrage of intrigue, strategies, and warfare. Yet scholars believe David wrote most of his poems (the Psalms) while under such conditions. David figured it out—his identity was in God. His success was defined by the level to which he was experiencing an intimate love relationship with God.

When given the opportunity, David never took up that spear to kill Saul (1 Samuel 18). His identity was not in being king. He wanted only what God wanted. He knew that if he used man's ways, Saul's ways, to become king, he would have defiled his core identity. David was already secure in God's love. He didn't need to be king. He didn't need a position. He didn't need the adulation of men. He was secure enough in his identity to know

God would accomplish His will through him as he delighted in His love.

> *Delight yourself in the LORD, and He shall give you the desires of your heart. Commit your way to the LORD, trust in Him, and He shall bring it to pass. Rest in the LORD, and wait patiently for Him; do not fret because of him who prospers in his way... the man who brings wicked schemes to pass. Cease from anger... do not fret—it only causes harm.*
> **Psalm 37: 4-8**

These are the words of one who knows God's love and delights in the reality of intimacy. David understood that if he learned to delight in God's love, God would, in turn, give him the heart desires of his work, his family, and his ministry.

So, in the busyness of your life, know that you are loved by God. Begin to tear down the artificial and phony that you have used to define success. Delight yourself in God. Redefine yourself as one beloved. This is what you were created for; this is what brings security and joy.

The Dangerous Excursion: Day 16

1. How would you define success in your life?

2. Are you experiencing God's love in your life? If so, what has been the reason? If not, why not?

3. What does it mean, in your own words, to be beloved of God?

DAY 17: PASSION

2 Samuel 6

11 The ark of the Lord remained in the house of Obed-Edom the Gittite three months. And the Lord blessed Obed-Edom and all his household.

12 Now it was told King David, saying, "The Lord has blessed the house of Obed-Edom and all that belongs to him, because of the ark of God." So David went and brought up the ark of God from the house of Obed-Edom to the City of David with gladness. 13 And so it was, when those bearing the ark of the Lord had gone six paces, that he sacrificed oxen and fatted sheep. 14 Then David danced before the Lord with all his might; and David was wearing a linen ephod. 15 So David and all the house of Israel brought up the ark of the Lord with shouting and with the sound of the trumpet.

16 Now as the ark of the Lord came into the City of David, Michal, Saul's daughter, looked through a window and saw King David leaping and whirling before the Lord; and she despised him in her heart. 17 So they brought the ark of the Lord, and set it in its place in the midst of the tabernacle that David had erected for it. Then David offered burnt offerings and peace offerings before the Lord.

20 Then David returned to bless his household. And Michal the daughter of Saul came out to meet David, and said, "How glorious was the king of Israel today, uncovering himself today in the eyes of the maids of his servants, as one of the base fellows shamelessly uncovers himself!"

21 So David said to Michal, "It was before the Lord, who chose me instead of your father and all his house, to appoint me ruler over the people of the Lord, over Israel. Therefore I will play music before the Lord. 22 And I will be even more undignified than this, and will be humble in my own sight. But as for the maidservants of whom you have spoken, by them I will be held in honor."
23 Therefore Michal the daughter of Saul had no children to the day of her death.

WORSHIPPER WARRIOR

It was the last day of a three-day personal retreat. My first two days had been spent alone in silence—reading, meditating on Scripture, hiking, and writing. I was mourning the loss of my job as a pastor. I had resigned from the church I deeply loved, and my heart needed time alone. I had come to seek the heart of Jesus and get perspective.

Now I stood in the icy white waters of the South Platte River. It was early morning, steam was rising off the eddies and the sun's rays were beginning to pierce through the ponderosa pines. The fading night was giving way to the rising sun, and the sky had turned from grey to peach to blue. All around me were cathedral-like canyon walls draped in the first signs of a new day.

Gripping my fly rod, I made my first cast and followed the fly through the ripples and curves of the fast-moving stream. Out of the shadows on the far bank, quietly and methodically, stepped a doe and her fawn. We stared at each other for a moment, then she took a drink. Both moved across the river without making a sound.

Suddenly, without warning, tears welled up. I began to sob.

Unable to stand, I walked over to the embankment and for the next hour all my pain, disappointment, and rage was unleashed. Something deep within was moving in my heart. I was reminded of something bigger and deeper within my soul, something I needed—something that needed to be healed within me.

Looking back, I recognized the ache of my soul and the beauty of God's heart in that moment. It was cleansing. It was the presence of God upon me. It was the passion of every man's heart—to find ourselves in the primeval touch of nature, wildness, and creation. I was rediscovering myself.

The word *passion* basically means "to be affected by." It is the fuel source of the soul,[104] something that gives us energy, a source for the desires of our heart. The fountainhead of passion is affected by what we see and feel. For me that morning, my passions were aroused, and my heart came alive as I experienced the river, the canyon, and the untouched beauty of God's magnificent work of art.

The passions of the heart capture the essence of our personhood. It is the core of our being as men. Yet we have been taught from childhood to disregard and even distrust our feelings. I didn't know just how deep my loss had been until I stepped into the river and felt the sensations of the beauty, majesty, and serenity of God being there. There was energy and it was piercing my heart. It was the presence of the living God.

Simon Weil had it partially right. He said there are only two things that pierce the human heart: beauty and affliction.[105] I would add one thing— the presence of God. The presence of God pierces our heart. For men in our culture, none of these are acceptable to acknowledge, but all are critical to finding our heart and discovering our passion. Passion is missing because our heart has never come alive.

David's heart was alive. David was wholehearted. David defined his identity through the love and intimacy he was experiencing in God. His passion was unleashed by his intimacy with God's presence. This identity had awakened his heart and the affect was joy, exuberance, and playfulness that pervaded his outlook. This is no clearer than the way David's response to the coming of the Ark of the Covenant into Jerusalem is described.

> *And so it was, when those bearing the ark of the Lord had gone six paces, that he sacrificed oxen and fatted sheep. Then David danced before the Lord with all his might; and David was wearing a linen ephod. So David and all the house of Israel brought up the ark of the Lord with shouting and with the sound of the trumpet. Now as the ark of the Lord came into the City of David, Michal, Saul's daughter, looked through a window and saw King David leaping and whirling before the Lord; and she despised him in her heart.*
> *2 Samuel 6: 13-16*

In ancient Israel, such rejoicing often accompanied major victories in battle. In every other instance, women are mentioned as dancing—not men and certainly not the king.[106] To be fair, Michal, his estranged wife, has the same reaction that most would have today. Imagine the senior pastor of your church acting like this during worship! This passionate display by David was unheard of and definitely countercultural, even in Israel. After studying David's life for many years, I'm convinced he did not plan it or prepare for what happened. David simply responded to the intense gratitude he suddenly felt as a result of God's love.

Gratitude and Joy

Think about what David has just gone through: from the wilderness as an outlaw to the throne as a king! From a war-torn battlefield to the peace of finally arriving in the beloved city of Jerusalem. I believe David's heart is deluged with sorrow, grief, joy, and gratitude. It's all there. His response? Dancing, spinning, whirling, pure unmanufactured emotion—a passionate appreciation for what God has done. It is a mixture of joy and gratitude.

In her research, Brené Brown discovered to her surprise that a key concept of wholehearted, healthy people is the relationship between gratitude and joy.

> Without exception, every person I interviewed who described living a joyful life, or who described themselves as joyful, actively practiced gratitude and attributed their joyfulness to their gratitude. Both joy and gratitude were described as spiritual practices that we bound to a belief in human connectedness and a power greater than us.[107]

For David, this joy overflowed from his deep gratitude for the work and presence of God. The Ark was not only the symbol of God's presence in the nation of Israel, it *was* most literally the place of God's dwelling.

A little history on the Ark of the Covenant: Wherever the Ark had rested, God's Presence had been manifested, either in great blessing or cursing (1 Samuel 4-5; 1 Chronicles 13:14). While the Lord was indeed present among His people, He chose to localize the manifest presence of His glory in the Ark. Exodus 15:22 reads, "There I will meet with you … on the ark of the testimony, I will speak with you." The people of Israel believed the closest encounter one could have with the living God was in proximity to the Ark.

David is acknowledging before the Lord the passion of one who is subject to the One he loves, the ultimate King of Israel! The psalmist refers to God as the "Shepherd [King] of Israel" who sits "enthroned between the cherubim" (Psalm 80:1), a direct reference to the Ark and the cherubim whose wings enfolded the top of the chest. This was the Ark of the King of Israel that had led the way in one military campaign after another (2 Kings 19:15; 6:2; Numbers 10:33-35). When they crossed the Jordan, the river stopped flowing (Joshua 3:13), and in Jericho the Presence of the Lord, represented by the Ark, led the people to victory (Joshua 6).

David's passion of gratitude and joy is enveloped in his conviction of the Lordship and Presence of Yahweh over his life! This passion overwhelmed and overcame him. David was experiencing the risen Lord over Israel, Jerusalem, his kingship, and himself.

Passion for Presence

Standing on a London street corner was G.K. Chesterton, the great author and philosopher. As the story goes, a newspaper reporter approached to discuss his recent conversion to Christianity.

> "May I ask you one question?" the reporter said.
>
> "Certainly," replied Chesterton.
>
> "If the risen Christ suddenly appeared at this very moment and stood behind you, what would you do?"
>
> Chesterton looked straight into the reporter's eyes and said, "He is."[108]

Was Chesterton using some mere figure of speech, espousing a dreamy mystical view of God in his life, or giving a knee-jerk response to a pesky reporter? Not at all. The philosopher was acknowledging the Presence of the risen Christ in his life! He believed it. The fruit of that conviction was borne out in his life from that day forward. Many critics have said he was the greatest writer of the twentieth century. One put it this way: "The reason he was the greatest writer of the twentieth century was because he was also the greatest thinker of the twentieth century."[109] Now we know what gave him his passion!

Arguably the most important truth of the Christian faith is the resurrection of Christ. Everything about our faith rises and falls on this conviction. But biblical theology's preoccupation with the risen Christ is too often seen only as an apologetic, rather than a personal experience. Yet the One Who walked the dusty roads of Galilee, Who laid hands on the sick, Who ate around the fire with His disciples, Who drank wine at weddings, Who laughed, Who cried, and Who loves you and me is alive now! He is risen! He is alive right now in New York, in California, in Japan, in China. The present risen Christ is on the earth today. The resurrected Jesus is standing next to you at this moment.

This is passion for the presence of the risen Jesus Christ. Former Catholic priest, bestselling author, and self-described struggling alcoholic Brennan Manning writes, "The most radical demand of Christian faith lies in summoning the courage to say yes to the present risenness of Jesus Christ."[110] In other words, the resurrection of Jesus must be experienced at this very moment. Jesus said, "Know that I am with you always" (Matthew 28:20). In the Greek, "always" can be translated "always!" He is.

Rumor of Angels

He is. Always available; always present, Jesus is. This is the ultimate passion of David; the ultimate passion of being wholehearted. This is indeed the deepest passion of the worshipper and warrior—the presence of the risen Christ moment by moment.

William Barry wrote, "We must school ourselves to pay attention to our experience of life in order to discern the touch of God or what Peter Berger calls the rumor of angels from all the other influences of our experience."[111] Living in the presence of Jesus daily is the passion that unlocks the doors of a new intimacy with Christ. When we discover this passion, our lives are transformed forever. The mundane is changed into the miraculous.

After a fateful flight from Tokyo to London, Liz and I had experienced one delay after another, arriving in London a full day later than we had planned. I found myself meeting with the head of Cathay Pacific to argue my case. Begrudgingly, he gave us new tickets to our final destination in Malaga, Spain. We were even given first-class seats! After being awake for over twenty-four hours, we were completely exhausted and only wanted a little sleep. But upon sitting down I could feel the nudging of the Lord for the man next to me. He was a Canadian Japanese, and upon hearing that we were living in Japan, he became animated in his discussion with me.

After an hour of small talk, I shared with him that I was a Christian missionary. The tempo and depth of our conversation abruptly changed as I shared more. Over the next few hours this businessman opened up to me that he had recently been through a divorce, was addicted to gambling, and just that day had contemplated suicide. As I shared how he could know and experience the risen Christ in his life, with tears in his eyes, he opened his heart to the presence of God! Sheer coincidence? I don't think so. He is.

I have shared several times in this book about my brokenness in the face of resigning at Mountain Springs Church; what I haven't shared is how I knew that God was moving me on. After being placed on sabbatical by the church board, I began to seek the Lord like never before. Liz and I fasted often, sought wise counsel, studied a dozen books, and read through the New Testament. But the most amazing evidence of the presence of the risen Christ was the phrase we kept hearing: "the road less traveled," spoken to us seven times in four months. We heard the phrase on the radio, through an interview of Robert Redford on TV, in a conversation with a noted pastor and mentor. It seemed like every other week or so we heard this phrase. It was God's voice to us. He was alive, with us, and we knew it.

WORSHIPPER WARRIOR

All you're living for can come alive when you discover the presence of the risen Christ is with you. Standing behind you. Riding in the seat next to you on your way to work. Walking on that trail alongside you. He is there.

We can let our circumstances use us, or we can use them. In my turbulent journey over the past two years, the greatest discovery has been that I can feed off my setbacks, gaining strength through being open and vulnerable about my sins, selfishness, and pride. By facing the shame and darkness, inviting the risen Christ to come, I am growing in maturity and faith. It is the way to wholeness. Through harmonizing the dark places of our heart with the presence of the risen Christ, He can transform us.

The Apostle Paul lived his life in the reality of the risen Christ. It was his daily experience that continually uplifted his heart in the face of unimaginable hardship, torment, and sorrow. Paul's very personality had been formed anew through his encounter with the risen Christ on the dusty road to Damascus (Acts 9). Later in life he described the passion of his heart when he wrote to the Galatians,

> *I have been crucified with Christ. My ego is no longer central. It is no longer important that I appear righteous before you or have your good opinion, and I am no longer driven to impress God. Christ lives in me. The life you see me living is not "mine," but it is lived by faith in the Son of God, who loved me and gave himself for me. I am not going to go back on that.*
> **Galatians 2: 20 MSG**

Paul's ego was the risen Christ. He had discovered the great passion of being crucified with Christ, experiencing His resurrection, and allowing Jesus to live in and through him. This is the passion of David. This is the growing passion of the worshipper and warrior.

Today, wherever you are—sitting at your desk at work, driving to the job, eating dinner alone or with your family, watching your daughter at ballet—know that Christ is there. He loves you. He wants to know you. He is.

The Dangerous Excursion: Day 17

1. Have you felt the presence of God in your life before? If so, when and where? What was it like?

2. Can you recall situations, "rumors of angels," that are only explainable by realizing that Jesus was there? When?

3. How can you live in the reality of the risen Christ this week?

DAY 18: COMPROMISE

2 Samuel 11

1 It happened in the spring of the year, at the time when kings go out to battle, that David sent Joab and his servants with him, and all Israel; and they destroyed the people of Ammon and besieged Rabbah. But David remained at Jerusalem.

2 Then it happened one evening that David arose from his bed and walked on the roof of the king's house. And from the roof he saw a woman bathing, and the woman was very beautiful to behold. 3 So David sent and inquired about the woman. And someone said, "Is this not Bathsheba, the daughter of Eliam, the wife of Uriah the Hittite?" 4 Then David sent messengers, and took her; and she came to him, and he lay with her, for she was cleansed from her impurity; and she returned to her house. 5 And the woman conceived; so she sent and told David, and said, "I am with child."

14 In the morning it happened that David wrote a letter to Joab and sent it by the hand of Uriah. 15 And he wrote in the letter, saying, "Set Uriah in the forefront of the hottest battle, and retreat from him, that he may be struck down and die." 16 So it was, while Joab besieged the city, that he assigned Uriah to a place where he knew there were valiant men. 17 Then the men of the city came out and fought with Joab. And some of the people of the servants of David fell; and Uriah the Hittite died also.

18 Then Joab sent and told David all the things concerning the war, 19 and charged the messenger, saying, "When you have finished telling the matters of the war to the king, 20 if it happens that the king's wrath rises, and he says to you: 'Why did you approach so near to the city when you fought? Did you not know that they would shoot from the wall? 21 Who struck Abimelech the son of Jerubbesheth? Was it not a woman who cast a piece of a millstone on him from the wall, so that he died in Thebez? Why did you go near the wall?'—then you shall say, 'Your servant Uriah the Hittite is dead also.'"

22 So the messenger went, and came and told David all that Joab had sent by him. 23 And the messenger said to David, "Surely the men prevailed against us and came out to us in the field; then we drove them back as far as the entrance of the gate. 24 The archers shot from the wall at your servants; and some of the king's servants are dead, and your servant Uriah the Hittite is dead also."

25 Then David said to the messenger, "Thus you shall say to Joab: 'Do not let this thing displease you, for the sword devours one as well as another. Strengthen your attack against the city, and overthrow it.' So encourage him."

26 When the wife of Uriah heard that Uriah her husband was dead, she mourned for her husband. 27 And when her mourning was over, David sent and brought her to his house, and she became his wife and bore him a son. But the thing that David had done displeased the Lord.

Over the past several years, many high-level, extremely successful leaders have mysteriously lost their way. Dominique Strauss-Kahn, former head of the International Monetary Fund and a former French politician, has been involved in several financial and sexual scandals. Before that, David Sokol, rumored to be Warren Buffett's successor, was forced to resign for trading in Lubrizol stock prior to recommending that Berkshire Hathaway purchase the company.[112]

Hewlett-Packard CEO Mark Hurd resigned for submitting false expense reports concerning his relationship with a contractor. U.S. Senator John Ensign resigned after covering up an extramarital affair with monetary payoffs. Lee B. Farkas, former chairman of giant mortgage lender Taylor, Bean & Whitaker, was found guilty for his role in one of the largest bank-fraud schemes in American history.[113] And who hasn't heard about the epic meltdowns of some of the most successful people in Hollywood and the media for all kinds of sexual impropriety? Harvey Weinstein, Matt Lauer, Charlie Rose … the list goes on and on.

In my city of Colorado Springs, several prominent pastors have lost their churches and reputations in high-stakes, unethical choices. In the 1990s, Colorado Springs was called the "mecca of evangelicalism," but everything has changed over the years as controversy has plagued our city.

What is going on? With so much at stake, with so much work and effort involved in reaching such high levels of success in their respective fields, why would these men risk everything for such shallow returns? Why do men risk their careers and unblemished reputations for such ephemeral gains?

It is the same question we must ask of King David. Two names are forever linked with his. Even those who are basically illiterate of the Scriptures know these two names. One is Goliath, the massive giant we covered early on in our book. But the second, just as infamous, is Bathsheba. The two could hardly be more different—the ugly, cruel, obstinate, prideful Goliath, and the stunning, gentle beauty Bathsheba.

Our story opens with the conditions of David's life. He is no longer an outlaw but the established king of Israel. He no longer calls caves his home but lives in a palace. Lesser wars are still being fought, but David has delegated his field command to Joab, and has chosen to enjoy the benefits of his labors.

David's army is headed out to battle—possibly for the first time without David. He is now well established as the king and has nothing more to prove. David has delegated much of his responsibilities to capable men. His chief of staff, Joab, has fought all the great battles beside David and is trustworthy. He is on the top of the org chart. Even Saul's house has submitted to his leadership. All of Israel is united under "the house of David." It's time to rest.

After all, kings in medieval times didn't risk their lives in low-level battles; the small gains were not worth risking their lives. As king, David has bigger, more visionary decisions to make. Besides, he can give orders and make decisions better ensconced in his penthouse office, his "Trump Tower." Staying home is just common sense.

Made for Mission

But common sense may not always be God sense. David is a worshipper and a warrior, and his power, his anointing, is rooted deeply in warfare. David's warrior conditions have, as we covered on Day Fifteen, been the context of his character formed in adversity—war, sexuality, and blood.

All this has formed the man; all this has kept David on guard and ready. David's attitudes toward life and godliness have been built upon the conditions of war and soldiering.

Is staying home a symptom of anemia of the soul? Has David grown bored with his own success? Has he lost the robust zest for life? Is he pulling back from the vibrant praise, the energetic prayers, the passionate worship of his earlier life?

As a pastor in a city whose economy is largely impacted by and built around the Air Force Academy and three other large military bases, I am regularly in contact with and counseling men in the military and those recently retired. The story I hear again and again is the loss of comradery and vision when men leave the service. Their entire adult life has been built around training, preparing for a mission to protect our nation. Without that mission and without the men they've grown accustomed to supporting, there is a loss of something deep within their heart.

Men, you were made for an energetic mission. You are called to a mission, and specifically an assignment from God (Day Six). John Eldredge has called it the warrior desire to be a hero. "The desire is there. Every man wants to play the hero. Every man needs to know that he is powerful."[114]

The problem is when our quest to be the hero and to be powerful moves into an arena of the flesh. David has a mission, and that mission has been abandoned. But replacing the mission gets David into deeper trouble.

Patterns

Sin is always crouching at the door ready to master us. The battle for our heart never changes. No matter our success yesterday, the culprit of our souls, Satan, is always looking for ways to pierce our hearts today. It is no mistake that Jesus mentioned the Giver of the wholehearted life and the destroyer of that life in the same sentence: *"The thief does not come except to steal, and to kill, and to destroy. I have come that they may have life, and that they may have it more abundantly*" (John 10:10). The choice to live the wholehearted life will be opposed.

What many don't realize in studying this story is the pattern of compromise that has followed David most of his adult life. Even though the flame of the Holy Spirit has descended upon him and met him in victory, even with the reality of God's intimacy and power undergirding his choices. With weariness and depression plaguing him at times, David has known where to go to find the green pastures and living streams of a loving relationship with God. He has risen to unbelievable success through the anointing of God, yet a pattern of compromise has followed—a pattern that either no one has noticed, or others have been unwilling to confront in him.

In Deuteronomy 17, God laid down three specific things a king in Israel was to abstain from. David, a man of the Scriptures, would have known these commands in the Pentateuch since childhood: "he shall not multiply horses to himself" (vs. 16); "neither shall he greatly multiply to himself silver and gold" (vs. 17); and the third was "neither shall he multiply wives to himself, that his heart would not turn away" (vs. 17).

David had adhered to the command concerning accumulating horses in battle. He had dedicated the gold and silver, bringing them to the temple in obedience to God's command.

But the one command most closely associated with the heart he has been compromising for years: David has been multiplying wives all along (note 1 Samuel 25; 2 Samuel 3:2-5). In addition to his multiple wives, as king, David also has been adding concubines to his harem (2 Samuel 5:13). David's pattern of sin has gone unnoticed to everyone but God.

The rendezvous with Bathsheba is the climax to a pattern of compromise in the heart of David. The man after God's own heart has a dark place, an unsubmitted portion within. There is ignorance of a pattern now being revealed. Some call it a blind spot. Some might say David is a target because of his success. Others would say the intoxication of continual accomplishment is his undoing. As Novartis chairman Daniel Vasella told *Fortune* magazine,

> For many of us the idea of being a successful manager—leading the company from peak to peak, delivering the goods quarter by quarter—is an intoxicating one. It is a pattern of celebration leading to belief, leading to distortion. When you achieve good results ... you are typically celebrated, and you begin to believe that the figure at the center of all that champagne-toasting is yourself.[115]

More David. Less God. For David, and for many who are extravagantly successful, the less we pay attention to God, the more we pad our own egos. The more we act like gods of our own lives. Eugene Peterson writes,

> The less David is paying attention to God, the more he's acting if he were God, acting like a god in relation to Bathsheba, pulling her into the orbit of his will.[116]

The way of sin is that it doesn't feel like sin at all. It feels great! It feels exhilarating. The Latin phrase *felix culpa*, attributed to Augustine (who knew much sexual sin), means "O happy sin."[117] When we sin, even knowing the harm it may cause, we feel like a god. We have control and power. Our hearts come alive.

But sin is like, as a friend told me years ago, "candy-coated shit." It starts off tasting awesome, but then the true taste takes over. There is a phenomenal measure of self-deception in sin. Our struggle in the twenty-first century may not be the "multiplying of horses," but it's definitely the multiplying of power—the same thing. Our struggle is not literally storing up gold and silver, but it is accumulation of wealth—the same thing. Our battle is not the "multiplying of wives," but it is the addictions to and fascination with sex—the same thing. Not much has really changed. For men, these are still our greatest temptations—power, money, and sex. The strategies of Satan may have a different look—from horses to plush corner offices, from gold to stock options, from wives to internet porn—but the temptations are just as robust with the identical goal: the killing of our heart and the destruction of our life.

Consequences

God is so patient with us. Psalm 92 indicates that God lets us flourish "like grass" even in our wickedness, but if there is no repentance, He moves in and unleashes judgment. For David, after years of compromise, after years of hiddenness, the veil will come off. This one choice, to have sex with a married woman—a woman he doesn't even know—will now lead to consequences he has never experienced (see 2 Samuel 12).

Amazing, isn't it? We have freedom to choose or walk away from sin, but we don't have freedom to control the consequences of our choices. Even as powerful and untouchable as David is, at the zenith of his career, the consequences of this one action will reverberate through the remaining years of his life—and for that matter, all time. His sin is forgiven, but the consequences will be horrific: An innocent child will die, a virtuous man will be murdered, later one of his sons will treat his sister just as David has treated Bathsheba, and another son will become a murderer and the usurper of his throne. David's life and heart will never be the same. One writer, speaking of David's life at this time, said,

> His sins are forgiven but the consequences he had to take! When God forgives us and restores us to favor, He uses the rod too, and life is never quite the same again. Oh yes, He restores His repentant child to fellowship, but sometimes a man has to drink the bitter cup; a forgiven man may still have to reap what he has sown.[118]

Just this week I was counseling a young man who had come to me several years ago broken and repentant over an affair he was involved in. Even though he did all the right things in breaking it off, the lingering affects upon his wife and children are still being felt. Another man, who has become a close friend, was convicted by the Holy Spirit of an affair he was enslaved to. He repented and went to counseling for several years. But to this day he and his wife still carry the lingering scars upon their hearts of that one sinful choice. Consequences cut deeply into our hearts. Forgiveness is available, but the repercussions can be harsh.

All of us carry scars upon our hearts from the sins of our past. It is inevitable with our humanness. In this life, our primary focus is not the *avoidance* of sin but rather, *recognition* of sin. The fact is, we will sin. But the reality of our own ego combined with demonic deception make sin multi-layered and compounded. We all have failed. We all have guilt and regret.

A Gospel Turn

But the great turn of the story is the entrance of David's pastor, Nathan, in 2 Samuel 12. Nathan shows up with truth and righteousness. Nathan preaches a sermon that David has no idea is a sermon—the best kind. Nathan does what every great preacher does, what Jesus did: He tells a story and gradually reels you in. And just like Jesus in many of his parables, God's name is never mentioned. Nathan simply tells a simple story about a rich man, a poor man, and a lamb. David is drawn in and outraged by the callousness of the rich man—and then, Nathan brings the hammer down.

> Then Nathan said to David, "You are the man!"
> **2 Samuel 12: 7**

This is the Gospel to all of us. You are the man! The Gospel story is never about someone else. It's truly about you and me. Eugene Peterson writes, "The Gospel is never a truth in general; it's always a truth in specific … it's always about actual persons, actual pain, actual trouble, actual sin: you, me; who you are and what you've done."[119] The Gospel is our story of selfishness, sin, and the quagmire we have created. But the larger story that enwraps our personal testimony is one of grace, love, forgiveness, and a second chance.

We certainly don't mind the stories about others and what they've done—but it's when we enter the story and see ourselves that the Gospel turn comes. It's all right here in our own story that we find Jesus. Not some distant fairy tale, but our own story of badness, betrayal, and battles lost. This then is the Gospel to us, the turning toward God when we would rather run. The grace of God is experienced in our guilt and defeat.

WORSHIPPER WARRIOR

The Gospel has come to David. His response to Nathan's preaching: "*I have sinned against the Lord*" (verse 13). No more stories of others; no more generalities; only the specifics of his own life. David's heart is broken and his spirit contrite.

This is one of the great redemptive episodes of the Bible. David truly turned from his sin and gave himself back to God. The word *repent* means to turn around, to do a 180. David does that. Psalm 51 is David's prayer of repentance for his sin with Bathsheba. No other chapter of the Bible captures the depth of repentance and sorrow for sin.

To read this poem of David in *The Message* is to massage our heart with both the heinous evil of our sins and the generous love of God. I certainly don't know what each of you carry within your hearts of self-reproach, shame, and remorse, but I know this—Jesus forgives, heals, and restores. You are His beloved.

As we close this chapter, I want you to take the next few minutes to read this beautiful poem to yourself, stanza by stanza, and at the end of each, pray it back to God. Make it your prayer this day.

Generous in love—God, give grace!
Huge in mercy—wipe out my bad record.
Scrub away my guilt,
soak out my sins in your laundry.
I know how bad I've been;
my sins are staring me down.
You're the One I've violated, and you've seen
it all, seen the full extent of my evil.
You have all the facts before you;
whatever you decide about me is fair.
I've been out of step with you for a long time,
in the wrong since before I was born.
What you're after is truth from the inside out.
Enter me, then; conceive a new, true life.
Soak me in your laundry and I'll come out clean,
scrub me and I'll have a snow-white life.
Tune me in to foot-tapping songs,
set these once-broken bones to dancing.
Don't look too close for blemishes,
give me a clean bill of health.

God, make a fresh start in me,
shape a Genesis week from the chaos of my life.
Don't throw me out with the trash,
or fail to breathe holiness in me.
Bring me back from gray exile,
put a fresh wind in my sails!
Give me a job teaching rebels your ways
so the lost can find their way home.
Commute my death sentence, God, my salvation God,
and I'll sing anthems to your life-giving ways.
Unbutton my lips, dear God;
I'll let loose with your praise.
Going through the motions doesn't please you,
a flawless performance is nothing to you.
I learned God-worship
when my pride was shattered.
Heart-shattered lives ready for love
don't for a moment escape God's notice.
Make Zion the place you delight in,
repair Jerusalem's broken-down walls.
Then you'll get real worship from us,
acts of worship small and large,
Including all the bulls
they can heave onto your altar!
Psalm 51 – MSG

The Dangerous Excursion: Day 18

1. **What aspect of this story of David can you personally relate to and why?**

2. **Do you see a pattern of compromise in your life that has the potential to ruin it?**

3. **Do you see a pattern of compromise in the arenas of power, wealth, and sex? Explain what's happening.**

DAY 19: SUFFERING

2 Samuel 15

10 Then Absalom sent spies throughout all the tribes of Israel, saying, "As soon as you hear the sound of the trumpet, then you shall say, 'Absalom reigns in Hebron!'" 11 And with Absalom went two hundred men invited from Jerusalem, and they went along innocently and did not know anything. 12 Then Absalom sent for Ahithophel the Gilonite, David's counselor, from his city—from Giloh—while he offered sacrifices. And the conspiracy grew strong, for the people with Absalom continually increased in number.

13 Now a messenger came to David, saying, "The hearts of the men of Israel are with Absalom."

14 So David said to all his servants who were with him at Jerusalem, "Arise, and let us flee, or we shall not escape from Absalom. Make haste to depart, lest he overtake us suddenly and bring disaster upon us, and strike the city with the edge of the sword."

15 And the king's servants said to the king, "We are your servants, ready to do whatever my lord the king commands." 16 Then the king went out with all his household after him. But the king left ten women, concubines, to keep the house. 17 And the king went out with all the people after him, and stopped at the outskirts. 18 Then all his servants passed before him; and all the Cherethites, all the Pelethites, and all the Gittites, six hundred men who had followed him from Gath, passed before the king.

2 Samuel 16

5 Now when King David came to Bahurim, there was a man from the family of the house of Saul, whose name was Shimei the son of Gera, coming from there. He came out, cursing continuously as he came. 6 And he threw stones at David and at all the servants of King David. And all the people and all the mighty men were on his right hand and on his left. 7 Also Shimei said thus when he cursed: "Come out! Come out! You bloodthirsty man, you rogue! 8 The Lord has brought upon you all the blood of the house of Saul, in whose place you have reigned; and the Lord has delivered the kingdom into the hand of Absalom your son. So now you are caught in your own evil, because

you are a bloodthirsty man!"

9 Then Abishai the son of Zeruiah said to the king, "Why should this dead dog curse my lord the king? Please, let me go over and take off his head!"

10 But the king said, "What have I to do with you, you sons of Zeruiah? So let him curse, because the Lord has said to him, 'Curse David.' Who then shall say, 'Why have you done so?'"

11 And David said to Abishai and all his servants, "See how my son who came from my own body seeks my life. How much more now may this Benjamite? Let him alone, and let him curse; for so the Lord has ordered him. 12 It may be that the Lord will look on my affliction, and that the Lord will repay me with good for his cursing this day." 13 And as David and his men went along the road, Shimei went along the hillside opposite him and cursed as he went, threw stones at him and kicked up dust. 14 Now the king and all the people who were with him became weary; so they refreshed themselves there.

David's life has taken a bitter turn. From the rooftop heights of his beautiful palace in the center of Jerusalem to the depths of the Kidron Valley leading out of the city. This is one of the saddest episodes in the Bible. David's flight from his son Absalom is the most tragic circumstance of his life. The most pathetic thing about the whole story is that David knows in his heart that he deserves what he's experiencing.

Sin begets sin. David's suffering has been caused by his own lack of love and compassion for his son Absalom. The rape of his daughter Tamar has led his son Absalom to murder his other son Amnon, which has led David to harden his own heart against Absalom. (See 2 Samuel 13-14 for the whole brutal story.)

David has experienced rejection before. He understands the ways of disappointment, sin, and death. But nothing could have prepared him for the betrayal of his own son. It was the most bitter cup David would ever drink.

This is the David who once said, "*my cup runs over,*" the cup of the intimate presence of God. At the time, he was toasting the beauty, the salvation, the faithfulness of God as his Shepherd (Psalm 23). But would David drink as deeply from the cup of suffering as he had from the cup of salvation?

There is a line of reasoning in our American Christianity that if we will "get saved," center our life around believing God for great things, have a big vision for our life, and give our money to the right TV or radio evangelist, we will be exempt from suffering. "Success Faith" means big bucks for speakers and authors. Our radio channels and cable networks are filled with messages from the religious lottery, betting on the jackpot of the miraculous. The offer: If we will just give more, pray more, and sign up to be on the mailing list, we just might discover the instant supernatural life.

But this is not the life of faith found in Scripture. As you well know by now, the life of David is not an ad for the trouble-free life. David's life is rather a biographical sketch of a dangerous man who experienced awesome heart intimacy with God in worship and obedience, and who also knew the deepest pangs of shame and sin. This is the life of the ragamuffin, the broken, the authentic. David, if he's anything, is a picture of the reality of holy and sinful choices.

Will David now drink of the bitter cup of betrayal and rejection? I believe this is the greatest trial of David's life. What will he do under the strain of almost complete rejection?

For many, and quite honestly, even most, the choice to blame God for suffering is the go-to answer. In no area have I counseled more distraught people than the arena of suffering. It's a tough row to hoe, for sure. It takes an unshakable faith in the goodness and love of God, coupled with a strong theological constitution. Few men have it.

Team David

David must walk back into the wilderness. Back to the old haunts, back to the caves, the wind, and the open camp fires. So much of David's character has been formed here. Such hardship formed David, and such agony will bring out the best in him; his heart will be recovered. Suffering will make

David a better man.

As David walked out of his most beloved city, the city he has built, the city that has for years enjoyed peace under his leadership, he must have looked around to see who was following him. A great company from the people of Israel? No. Our passage reads, "The hearts of the men of Israel [were] with Absalom" (2 Samuel 15:13). His family? His mighty army? Nope. Where were all the people who had been so excited at his coronation? None came out on that Kidron Valley road. Instead he looks around and sees a ragtag group of foreigners, servants, and ruffians. "Then all his servants passed before him; and all the Cherethites, all the Pelethites, and all the Gittites, six hundred men who had followed him from Gath, passed before the king."[120] This is the team that's left? After all the years, all the victories, this is Team David?

Yes, it is, and you know what? This is the *best* group of men David could have assembled. Quite frankly, this is the A Team. This is David's Delta Force. These were the men who had been with him through the most dangerously difficult times of his life. These were truly bloodstained allies. These were the mighty men described in 2 Samuel 23 and 1 Chronicles 12. They had been with David in Gath, wilderness strongholds, and Engedi. They had endured battles, in hunger, in thirst. They had suffered with David. This was exactly the army of men he needed.

The phrase "David and his men" is used over twenty times in the two Books of Samuel. It's no mistake. David always needed his men. They were with him constantly in everything he did. David had suffered with these men, and they with him. In the struggles of life, they had seen David's reactions, his integrity, his faithfulness, his love *and* his sin. They knew about Bathsheba, Uriah (indeed Uriah was one of David's mighty men!), the death of the baby, the drama of David's household—yet whatever David's fate, they were going to share it. They refused to join the betrayers and desert him. Rather they chose to identify with their king in his most difficult time. Stephen Ambrose writes of the group that fought together through Normandy and the last year of World War II, "Within

Easy Company they had made the best friends they had ever had or would ever have. They were prepared to die for each other; more important, they were prepared to kill for each other."[121] An accurate description of David's mighty men.

Suffering brings out the best and worst in men. One of my favorite professors in graduate school, Dr. Robert Clinton, once said in a lecture that "suffering shows the heart of a man, what comes out in hardship is who he really is." I never forgot that. David's muscular, rough, scarred men knew the man they were following. They trusted him, and he trusted them.

Once, during a very low point in my life, a well-meaning friend said, "Steve, you don't really know Jesus is all you need until Jesus is all you have." I know she meant well. But to be honest, I really don't agree with the statement. Maybe that's heretical since it's one of those statements I've heard from many famous Christian writers. But I don't like it. I don't think it's accurate.

Don't get me wrong. Jesus *is* all we need for salvation! When it comes to the cross, the empty tomb, and blood sacrifice of Christ for our sins, Jesus is absolutely the only way, truth, and life! But I don't believe that most of the time, if we are walking through this life as Jesus' disciples, we should be suffering alone! I don't believe "Jesus is all you have!" I believe Jesus *and* brothers are all you have! Jerry Bridges said it well:

> There are many elements that go into the total concept of fellowship, as it is described in the New Testament, but the sharing together in suffering is one of the most profitable. It probably unites our hearts together in Christ more than any other aspect of fellowship.[122]

Men, in our greatest torment, in our darkest hour, we need bloodstained allies who will not desert us. Yes, we need Jesus—but we need Jesus with scarred skin on. David has that, and it becomes a key aspect of his recovery. If you don't have such men, then you need to cultivate them. As I stated on Day Nine (Allies), you need men who will not cut and run when difficulties come. You need men who have bled, been broken, and walked with you through despair. You need an A Team.

Humility

The true test of David's heart is what he does next. In the face of his darkest hour, abandoned by fair-weather friends, fired from his job, running for his life, he has a choice. Suffering always provides us with a choice: Surrendering to God in humility or surviving through self-effort and pride. David chooses humility. David is recovering the heart he had lost. The past few years had been difficult because David had lost his way. John Baillie said, "Humility is the obverse side of self-confidence in God, whereas pride is the obverse side of confidence in self."[123] David's pride and arrogance were on display, and now his recovery will be evident. As Shimei curses him along the road (2 Samuel 16:5-14), David reaches down and finds his humility.

As Shimei preaches to David, the presence of God comes. David sees his sinfulness for what it is, an affront to God's holiness. One author defines humility as "honestly assessing ourselves in light of God's holiness and our sinfulness."[124] David understands his pride in a new way, and he recovers his heart in the process.

True lasting recovery begins with humility. It's the opposite of modern psychology and self-help books. We have come to believe that God helps those who help themselves. Humility is recognizing that God helps those who humble themselves! The prophet Isaiah tells us what God is looking for in a man.

> *Says the Lord.*
> *"But on this one will I look:*
> *On him who is humble and of a contrite spirit ..."*
> **Isaiah 66: 2**

God is searching for men who desire to walk humbly with Him. Humility draws the gaze of God. Listen to the words of James: "God ... gives grace to the humble" (James 4:6). Contrary to our American worldview, it's not those who help themselves, but those who humble themselves who receive God's mercy and grace.

This is the power and promise of humility. God is personally involved with the man who chooses humility. God pours out grace, and the man who will surrender to God's love and power can experience it. It's as if humility acts as a magnet to capture God's attention and invite his grace and love into our lives.

Prayer

In suffering, David rediscovers the power of prayer! The subscript to Psalm 3 reads, "A Psalm of David when he fled from Absalom." David, in the chaos of exiting Jerusalem, mustering his faithful men, and finding a cave to hide in, makes time to pray. This psalm is David's prayer,

> *Lord, how they have increased who trouble me!*
> *Many are they who rise up against me.*
> *Many are they who say of me,*
> *"There is no help for him in God." Selah*
> ***Psalm 3: 1-2***

David is hammered by the accusations of enemies from within and without, echoing the sermon of Shimei, "David, there's no help from God! What are you thinking? God's done with you! You've screwed up one too many times!" Satan, the accuser, is bombarding David's thoughts. His detractors and those who have betrayed him are the spokespersons for the enemy.

Notice what David is doing in recovering his heart: He is being completely honest before the Lord. He is not listening to himself but preaching to himself. David's prayer is saying back to the Lord what his enemies are saying to him. David is thoroughly sharing his heart with God.

The chaos of our pain and suffering is where prayer begins. That's the point of being human. Getting in touch with our Creator in honest dialogue and intimacy. We must bare our very struggles to the Lord in honesty before we begin to accept His grace and love into our situations. It is at the heart of our pain that we discover a listening and caring God.

But You, O Lord, are a shield for me,
My glory and the One who lifts up my head.
I cried to the Lord with my voice,
And He heard me from His holy hill. Selah
Psalm 3: 3 – 4

At this point, a civil war is raging all around David (2 Samuel 17). Absalom's forces are engaging David's, and the old, battered, battle-tested general is putting back into place the secret to his success: strategy bathed in prayer. After countless surprise victories and narrow escapes, David knows God must be his shield, his breastplate, his greaves, his defender. David is in recovery. David is at his best in desperation.

Men, in our suffering, in our darkest hours, in our most vulnerable times, we must have strategy birthed in prayer. Over the years, in days of indecision and suffering, taking a prayer walk, clearing my head and heart and talking to the Lord has, more than anything else, enabled me to hear from God. I have received revelation for marriage, family, and work during prayer walks. Walking and talking with God. David has a strategy birthed in prayer.

I lay down and slept;
I awoke, for the Lord sustained me.

I will not be afraid of ten thousands of people
Who have set themselves against me all around.

Arise, O Lord;
Save me, O my God!
For You have struck all my enemies on the cheekbone;
You have broken the teeth of the ungodly.

Salvation belongs to the Lord.
Your blessing is upon Your people. Selah
Psalm 3: 5 - 8

David is experiencing a metamorphosis as he prays. Through bloodstained allies, through humility, and through prayer, God is driving fear out of David's life. From the guttural cries of his trouble to a good night's sleep? Such is the power and beauty of God when we most depend on Him. Faith is being reignited in David. The Spirit has come and ministered to him. In prayer, in honesty, in crying out, David is a transformed man. His faith is back. David stands in the vortex of peace and beauty while a storm rages around him. Tim Keller describes the beauty and delight of God in suffering:

> Jonathan Edwards once said: "God is glorified not only by His glory's being seen, but by its being rejoiced in." It is not enough to say, "I guess he is God, so I have got to knuckle under." You have to see his beauty. Glorifying God does not mean obeying him only because you have to. It means to obey him because you want to—because you are attracted to him, because you delight in him. This is what C. S. Lewis grasped and explained so well in his chapter on praising. We need beauty.[125]

David has never lost his trust and attraction to God. God is back in David's life, at the center of his heart. Through prayer, through deep suffering, David is recovering his worshipping and warring heart!

With Jesus

In this lament, somewhere in a cave in the wilderness of Ephraim outside Jerusalem, David prophesies the suffering of Jesus. As a matter of geography, David "went up by the Ascent of the Mount of Olives" (2 Samuel 15:30). Right here, possibly in the very spot, is the Garden of Gethsemane. David just might have walked through the very garden. For it would be here at the base of the Valley of Kidron (1 Samuel 15:23-30), among the ancient olive trees, that one thousand years later, Jesus would weep before His Father and cry out, *"Father, if it is your will, take this cup from Me; nevertheless not My will but Yours be done"* (Luke 22:42). In the following days Jesus would experience the deepest agony, betrayal, and torture known to man.

As one growing to be a worshipper and warrior, how will we navigate suffering? Just as many Christ-followers get cancer as those who don't. There doesn't seem to be proportionally fewer believers in hospitals than those who don't follow Christ. Jesus said, "He makes His sun rise on those who are evil and on those who are good, and makes the rain fall on the righteous [those who are morally upright] and the unrighteous [the unrepentant, those who oppose Him]."[126]

But, when we, the Jesus-followers, suffer, we enter into a new dimension of the life of Christ. The worshipper and warrior is one who has suffered *with* Christ. Stephen Smith has written, "To grow in the Jesus life is to grow through suffering, not around it."[127] We can walk into the valley of the shadow of death because He has. Isaiah even describes the character of Jesus from the perspective of His suffering:

> *He was despised and rejected by mankind,*
> *a man of suffering, and familiar with pain.*
> *Like one from whom people hide their faces*
> *he was despised, and we held him in low esteem.*
> **Isaiah 53: 3**

To drink to the dregs the bitter cup of suffering—sickness, divorce, betrayal, cancer, firing, failure—is to identify with "a man of suffering, and familiar with pain." Jesus is with you in suffering, especially in suffering! He experienced it all. Jesus is mystically there in our suffering. It's His familiar ground. We can bring Christ into our betrayals, for He was betrayed. We can invite Christ into our agony because He was tortured and beaten on our behalf.

In the early 1900s, Amy Carmichael was busy rescuing children in India from temple prostitution. The care of these orphans demanded everything she had. Yet because of a debilitating injury, she spent the last twenty years of her life confined to a bed in Calcutta. Her work never stopped—and even thrived—as she guided the ministry from her bed of pain. Once while writing a friend, she wrote of suffering,

> *They are battle wounds. They are signs of high confidence—*
> *honours. The Father holds His children very close to His heart when*
> *they are going through such rough places as this.*
> **I Peter 2: 21 NIV**

Peter, who watched the torture of Christ, would later write, "*To this you were called, because Christ suffered for you, leaving you an example, that you should follow in his steps.*"[128] Christ is with us in our deepest suffering, for it is the life He chose in order to redeem us and set us free from sin.

Jesus, the original worshipper and warrior, is with us, at home next to us, in our darkest nights.

It is through suffering that we can meet Christ in the most profound ways. When we humble ourselves, cry out, and follow in His steps in such wilderness times, through the loneliness, and in such heartbreak, we discover Jesus and His wounds in a profound way. While confined to her bed, Amy Carmichael penned these words,

Hast thou no scar?
No hidden scar on foot, or side, or hand?
I hear thee sung as mighty in the land;
I hear them hail thy bright, ascendant star.
Hast thou no scar?

Hast thou no wound?
Yet I was wounded by the archers; spent,
Leaned Me against a tree to die; and rent
By ravening beasts that compassed Me, I swooned.
Hast thou no wound?

No wound? No scar?
Yet, as the Master shall the servant be,
And piercéd are the feet that follow Me.
But thine are whole; can he have followed far
Who hast no wound or scar?[129]

The Dangerous Excursion: Day 19

1. Are you suffering right now? How is God wanting you to process the struggles you are experiencing?

2. What are your "battle scars" that have taught you deeper lessons of being wholehearted?

DAY 20: POET

2 Samuel 23
1 Now these are the last words of David.
  Thus says David the son of Jesse;
  Thus says the man raised up on high,
  The anointed of the God of Jacob,
  And the sweet psalmist of Israel:
2 "The Spirit of the Lord spoke by me,
  And His word was on my tongue.
3 The God of Israel said,
  The Rock of Israel spoke to me:
  'He who rules over men must be just,
  Ruling in the fear of God.
4 And he shall be like the light of the morning when the sun rises,
  A morning without clouds,
  Like the tender grass springing out of the earth,
  By clear shining after rain.'

It was autumn in the Rocky Mountains. I was surrounded by an ancient aspen grove, alone among towering trees that seemed to reach into the heavens. Their golden leaves danced and fluttered in the autumn breeze. A sculpture in motion, like a snowstorm of golden shavings dropping from the sky, the woods were filled with ripened leaves falling. All around me, throughout the forest, the dark moist earth was being repainted in a thick golden carpet. Poetry in action. Though I had come to hunt elk, I was transfixed. The beauty was enough to take my breath away. I was reminded of the hauntingly elegant poem of Robert Frost,

> O hushed October morning mild,
> Thy leaves have ripened to the fall;
> Tomorrow's wind, if it be wild,
> Should waste them all.

The crows above the forest call;
Tomorrow they may form and go.
O hushed October morning mild,
Begin the hours of this day slow.
Make the day seem to us less brief.
Hearts not averse to being beguiled,
Beguile us in the way you know.[130]

That morning, and many mornings in the fall when I am in the woods, I'm beguiled. For it is in creation, walking in the poem and sculpture of God, that I have often rediscovered God's love and character. Some of my most intimate times with God have been sitting alone in his creation poetry. John Eldredge said it this way: "Creation is epic and intimate. [God] is epic and intimate. Everywhere around me, an obsession with beauty and attention to detail." The artist is revealed by his creation—his music, his paintings, his poetry. God's artwork speaks of Who He is. God is obsessed with majesty, color, and diversity. The sheer enormity of the work defines the character of the Great Artist.

Think of the ocean and its beauty and mystery. Meditate on the mountains and their enormous peaks and deep dark valleys. Walk through the woods at night in the middle of a thunderstorm! God is wild, God is majestic, God is beautiful, God is untamable.

> *But the basic reality of God is plain enough. Open your eyes and there it is! By taking a long and thoughtful look at what God has created, people have always been able to see what their eyes as such can't see: eternal power, for instance, and the mystery of his divine being.*
> **Romans 1: 19-20 MSG**

The Divine Poet

God is the Divine Poet. His mysterious and loving ways are painted upon the trees, the leaves, and the wind. Men, we were created by God to know God through the wild ways, His extravagant poetry in creation. You and I came from the dust of the earth. At our core, we as men are earthy. It is our destiny and our calling to know and worship The Artist and be filled with His poetry.

As David's life is nearing the end, how fitting and right that he would pen one last poem. The poet king, the worshipper warrior, gives us what many poets have given us at the end of their lives—an epithet poem. For Frost it was "The Road Not Taken." For Keats it was the sad, desperate words, "whose name was writ in water." For David, it was a poem of imagination, the creative way of the wholehearted.

It's interesting that David, in his poetic last will and testament of praise, never mentions his position as king, sovereign, or commander. David focuses on the man he has become through the intimacy with God he has discovered. David's identity is "the sweet psalmist of Israel." David viewed his greatest contribution to his nation to be as a poet worshipper and warrior. David's life, with all the same battles we fight and struggles we experience, lived out as a poet, is the song of the wholehearted man who has discovered the complexity and creativity of a life well lived.

Poetry is not in vogue these days. We live in a world where the deadline is causing us to flatline. Our hearts don't come alive with packed appointments and spreadsheets. Ours is a world of reduced speech, reduced life, and thus, a reduced heart. We are viewed as machines in the corporate world and as refined animals in a Darwinistic social world. Our language today speaks of the worldview we are forced to embrace. Individuals, families, and churches are often defined as "dysfunctional." Recently I asked our staff what the word *dysfunction* conjured up in their minds. The answers ranged from "unhealthy" to "the machinery we use." There are dysfunctional machines and hardware. A dysfunctional person is an oxymoron. People may be unhealthy, but they are not dysfunctional. We are not machines.

Even the Gospel in most of our churches is reduced to simplistic answers, old habits, and recycled platitudes. It is truth flattened, trivialized, and thus rendered powerless. Not unlike the movie *Honey, I Shrunk the Kids*, the question of our culture is, "Who shrunk manhood?" The answer is: We did, the church did, the culture did. But David, the man, is anything but trivial.

David's robust, wholehearted, fully human life, was a poetic life lived in a prose world. As I define the poetic, I am speaking of imagination and creativity put to wholehearted living. The poet is one who approaches the static, defined world with authenticity—gritty, real, and lived to capture all the nuances of an intimate relationship with God. The poet comes with mystery, reality, and a beauty that touches the depths of one's heart—the heartache, the passion, the presence of God. This is exactly what Jesus did. The people would say of Jesus that He didn't speak as the Pharisees, for He spoke with authority. The Poet Jesus came to recover our heart, our imagination, our humanity. David exemplifies such a life. Walter Brueggeman captured the heart of the poet:

> To address the issue of a truth greatly reduced requires us to be poets that speak against a prose world ... By prose I refer to a world that is organized in settled formulae, so that even pastoral prayers and love letters sound like memos. By poetry I do not mean rhyme, rhythm, or meter, but language that moves like Bob Gipson's fast ball, that jumps at the right moment, that breaks open old worlds with surprise, abrasion, and pace.[131]

At the very center of your Bible are the Psalms, the poems of a fiery, worshipful heart. A man fully alive; a man who experienced the intimacy of God in prayer and praise. David's poetic voice came, not from a formula, but from a river of love flowing through his heart.

Sons of God

Now don't get me wrong, I'm not saying that we as men are going to become poets and songwriters like David. I've never written a poem worth reading or penned a song worth singing. The Davidic poet that I'm speaking of is the man who has discovered his heart and has found the imagination of God flowing through his work, his marriage, his parenting. This is the poet that changes the world. This is part of the legacy of David—he reimagined intimacy with God, he was consumed with God, he was enraptured by God! Maybe it was what Walt Whitman was conjuring in his imagination, even as he lived in the reduced life of the Industrial Revolution at the turn of the nineteenth century:

After the seas are cross'd (as they seem already cross'd)
After the great captains and engineers have accomplish'd their work,
After the noble inventors, after the scientists, the chemist, the
geologist,   ethnologist,
Finally shall come the poet worthy of that name,
The true son of God shall come singing his songs.[132]

We as men, as sons of God, are called to be such poets, men who bring the creativity and innovation of the Great Poet into our lives and the lives of those we love, through our steady, hardy, masculine heart that is so largely missing in our reductionistic world. A culture that has defined manhood to something like the popular TV commercial of the inept male who can't believe his wife got better car insurance than he did, even as his wife speaks with a male voice. Wow, that's inspiring!

Our culture wants to shut our hearts down! To keep us quiet. To shut out the poetry of our souls. To push us into isolation and a secret life devoid of God. And so, we lose the heroic, the inspiring, the epic, the poetic. Thoreau, writing from a cabin deep in the New England woods, said, "The mass of men lead lives of quiet desperation. What is called resignation is confirmed desperation. From the desperate city you go."[133] The desperation is the loss of our masculine hearts.

The Bible is largely a Book of the sons of God who came as poets to a flattened, dead world and reinvisioned the Kingdom of God as life, joy, praise, and hope. It's Moses singing his song of liberation after the crossing of the Red Sea; it's Isaiah's entire prophetic warning to the nation of Israel; it's Jeremiah's lament; Solomon's Proverbs, and even the Apostle John in his apocalyptic poem at the end of the Book. It's the life of praise and worship, the theme John so captured in writing, "*the kingdom of the world has become the Kingdom of our Lord and of His Christ, and He shall reign forever and ever.*"[134]

The worshipper and warrior comes to a compressed, economized, scaled-down culture that is longing for more! The worshipper is one who brings praise to the analytical, prayers to the hopeless, and invites us to the rapture of loving God with all our heart, mind, body, and soul. In other words, a God we can know, not just one we can apologetically prove, or a technique we can practice. He is a Person to love, talk to, share our heart with. It's letting God be God in our life.

The story of David is that of a man who discovered and experienced the poetry of God in his heart. He allowed God to deal with him even as he dealt with God. He did it in real time with real problems. No hermit in a cave. The theme of his life is imagination, innovation, and creativity because—and don't miss this—he had given his heart fully to God. His praise, his worship, and his prayers were a connection to the imagination, innovation, and creativity of God. He tapped into the Fountainhead.

Jesus said it this way: "*If anyone thirsts, let him come to me and drink. Rivers of living water will brim and spill out of the depths of anyone who believes in me this way.*"[135] It is in tapping into the Fountainhead that we find life, for life flows from Him! The robust poetry of our soul flows from the robust life of the Poet Jesus!

Warrior Poets

Last fall we had our first men's conference, Wholeheart Advance, a ministry of Worshipper Warrior. Our theme and challenge was for men to discover intimacy with God through growing in and learning about wholehearted living. I spoke on such topics as shame, the false self, living dangerously, bloodstained allies, and how to charge into the life of being wholehearted. After the conference, one of the men gave me a poem he had written, his prayer to grow in being a wholehearted disciple of Jesus.

> Help me Lord to be wholehearted.
> Lead me to the secret place of my heart to meet you there,
> I want to shed light in the dark and stony places of my heart,
> To free me up to lead a wholehearted life.
>
> Lead me to love, lead me to be, lead me to live, wholeheartedly!
> I want to be free to love the way that you love,
> I want to see things the way that you see them.
> I want the eyes of my heart to be fully awakened,
> And to live a wholehearted life.

> A wholehearted life is a life fully alive with you.
> I want to be like David, whose heart was completely after yours,
> Show me how to live wholeheartedly in today's world,
> To live a life fully alive and fully wholehearted with you.
> I give you my heart to be fully wholehearted![136]

This poem was written by a son of God who had never written a poem before. But God had touched the deepest passions of his heart, and what came forth was a poem! Imagine that. Yes, imagine. His prayer to God, word smithed in the creative power of God working in his soul. He imagined God in a new way and found solace in a poem.

All of us are sons of God with poetry coursing through our spiritual veins. Randall Wallace, the screenwriter of the 1995 film Braveheart, gave a poetic tribute to the men of Scotland who bled and died on the fields of Bannockburn in the final narration of that epic movie:

> In the year of our Lord 1314, patriots of Scotland, starving and outnumbered, charged the fields at Bannockburn. They fought like warrior poets. They fought like Scotsmen, and won their freedom.

Such words might be a poetic tribute to David. Might these words be a poetic tribute to you!? Yes, you! Are you starving and outnumbered in your quest for God? Are you ready to charge the gates of Hell in your heart? Will you fight like a warrior poet for your freedom? A warrior poet fights through the forces of shame, religious posturing, and a false sense of security into the intimacy and creativity of loving with our whole heart.

It is ultimately what you do with your heart that determines your destiny. This is the only earthly life we have to live. To find the poem of your heart is to find God; to find God is to find the poem of your heart. He has made you and me each unique; penned upon our heart is the poem of God. Paul understood this when he wrote,

> *For by grace you have been saved through faith, and that not of yourselves; it is the gift of God, not of works, lest anyone should boast. For we are His workmanship, created in Christ Jesus for good works, which God prepared beforehand that we should walk in them.*
> ***Ephesians 2: 2 – 10***

The Greek word for "workmanship" is *poema*, the same root word for "poem." You are His poem! You are His work, created in the grace of God, by the love of God to show forth the works of a Poet God. Your life has been created by the Master Poet to be a poem of His expression lived out through your life. You were made a "little lower than the angels" with the fingerprint of God upon your soul.

As I'm writing this chapter, I'm sitting by a blazing fire with a fierce wind ripping through the trees surrounding me. The intensity of the wind and the bitter cold front that is marching into the forest is whipping up my fire. It feels poetic; it feels prophetic. The wind of God's Spirit is whipping up a fire in my heart. I can feel it. My hands are getting numb as the cold, brisk breeze is cascading across my laptop. But as I huddle closer to the fire, I'm energized by the effect. I can discern the presence of God wrenching at my heart. God is here.

Men, go to war. In a static, flattened world that has defined you as a cog in the system, don't forget you were created to be a work of art. You are a man. You are created by The Warrior Poet to be a worshipper and warrior. Fight for your freedom. Battle for your heart, knowing you possess the genetic code of God imprinted upon your soul. This is your time. This is your cry for freedom!

The Dangerous Excursion: Day 20

Reread the last two paragraphs. What's God stirring in your heart?

DAY 21: LEGACY

2 Samuel 23

8 These are the names of the mighty men whom David had: Josheb-Basshebeth[a]the Tachmonite ... he had killed eight hundred men at one time. 9 And after him was Eleazar the son of Dodo ... 10 He arose and attacked the Philistines until his hand was weary, and his hand stuck to the sword. The Lord brought about a great victory that day; and the people returned after him only to plunder. 11 And after him was Shammah the son of Agee the Hararite. The Philistines had gathered together into a troop where there was a piece of ground full of lentils. So the people fled from the Philistines. 12 But he stationed himself in the middle of the field, defended it, and killed the Philistines. So the Lord brought about a great victory.

13 Then three of the thirty chief men went down at harvest time and came to David at the cave of Adullam. And the troop of Philistines encamped in the Valley of Rephaim. 14 David was then in the stronghold, and the garrison of the Philistines was then in Bethlehem. 15 And David said with longing, "Oh, that someone would give me a drink of the water from the well of Bethlehem, which is by the gate!" 16 So the three mighty men broke through the camp of the Philistines, drew water from the well of Bethlehem that was by the gate, and took it and brought it to David. Nevertheless he would not drink it, but poured it out to the Lord. 17 And he said, "Far be it from me, O Lord, that I should do this! Is this not the blood of the men who went in jeopardy of their lives?" Therefore he would not drink it. These things were done by the three mighty men.

20 Benaiah was the son of Jehoiada ... He had killed two lion-like heroes of Moab. He also had gone down and killed a lion in the midst of a pit on a snowy day. 21 And he killed an Egyptian, a spectacular man. The Egyptian had a spear in his hand; so he went down to him with a staff, wrested the spear out of the Egyptian's hand, and killed him with his own spear ...

In the final words of the final chapter of the life of David, we find the legacy of the sweet psalmist of Israel. All that remains, that which will be left behind, of the now-aged warrior, worshipper, and poet, is found here. Written by the finger of God, contained in the Word of God—not unlike the etchings on a tombstone, or the final will and testament, a trust as it were, to the family of David and the people of Israel.

So much could have been written in this concluding chapter—the mighty exploits of David, for sure. Why didn't the author remind us of great battles won against Goliath, the Philistines, and the Amalekites? The downfall of Saul and the rise of the kingdom of David, why not write about that? Would it not be appropriate to include the riches and peace that have come to the nation because of David's leadership? None are mentioned.

What is David's legacy? What is contained here? The most human, robust, fiery, man in the Bible. We have it all. We have studied and journeyed together for three weeks, looking at all aspects of the man—his determination, his resolute heart, and his mistakes. At the end of a life, how do we define his legacy?

Mighty Warriors

I love the Bible! I love the adventurous story of David. I believe the God who makes no mistakes, the Author and Finisher of our faith, has given us the secret to David's life and the great legacy of a life well lived. Certainly, one could argue that David's intimacy and heart with and for God is the hallmark of his life. He is the original worshipper and warrior. But when we turn the pages of Scripture, as we look into the legacy that marked the man, it is all found right here in this chapter: "these are the names of the mighty warriors whom David had."[137] David's greatest legacy isn't just the love he possessed for God, but the men he left behind. The Great Author must have thought so, too. The individual names are found here. Their exploits, not David's, are recounted.

What an amazing tribute to David that these men are called "mighty warriors." They were certainly anything but that when he met them. When these men came to David in a wilderness cave some fifty years before, they were a band of ruffians and outlaws—distressed, discontented

201

debtors—and the Scriptures say, "he became captain over them" (1 Samuel 22:1-2). David transformed these outcast fugitives into fearsome men who loved God and loved David. Their exploits read like an action-hero movie.

What? Are you serious? This is no fictional Hollywood superhero Avengers movie script. These men really lived. These warriors actually did what is recorded here. I would love to have Josheb-Basshebeth by my side, even if I can't pronounce his name! After the description of "the three" and the "captains of the three," then the names are given of some thirty-seven others; their mighty deeds are not even recounted. It feels like the author just ran out of parchment; he had made his point. The heroics of the inner leadership recounted were only a snippet of what all these men did for David! It's one of the most daring, lionhearted, masculine passages in the entire Bible! Here it is for all to read and behold.

Here contained is David's legacy of men he ran with, did life with, gave his heart to, and obviously deeply loved. It's a legacy of love, daring courage, forgiveness, and longevity through the men he left behind. David never quit on his men, and his men never quit on David.

As he moved through each town, ministering to the masses, even thousands at a time, Jesus made it his highest priority to choose men, warriors, whom He could pour his heart and life into. Even with multitudes pressing in around him, Jesus was looking, searching, scouring the crowd for men he could disciple, mentor, and raise up.

> Then He went out again by the sea; and all the multitude came to Him, and He taught them. As He passed by, He saw Levi the son of Alphaeus sitting at the tax office. And He said to him, "Follow Me." So he arose and followed Him. Now it happened, as He was dining in Levi's house, that many tax collectors and sinners also sat together with Jesus and His disciples; for there were many, and they followed Him ... Again, the next day, John stood with two of his disciples. And looking at Jesus as He walked, he said, "Behold the Lamb of God!" The two disciples heard him speak, and they followed Jesus ... They came and saw where He was staying, and remained with Him ... One of the two who heard John speak, and followed Him, was Andrew, Simon Peter's brother. He first found

his own brother Simon, and said to him, "We have found the Messiah" (which is translated, the Christ). And he brought him to Jesus … The following day Jesus wanted to go to Galilee, and He found Philip and said to him, "Follow Me." Now Philip was from Bethsaida, the city of Andrew and Peter. Philip found Nathanael and said to him, "We have found Him of whom Moses in the law, and also the prophets, wrote—Jesus of Nazareth, the son of Joseph … Come and see."
Mark 2

What a motley crew! Not unlike the men chosen by David. Fisherman, tax collectors, and sinners. A.B. Bruce, who has written arguably the most in-depth book on how Jesus trained his disciples, described them by saying:

> At the time of their call they were exceedingly ignorant, narrow-minded, superstitious, full of Jewish prejudices, misconceptions, and animosities. They had much to unlearn of what was bad, and they were slow both to learn and unlearn … [they] needed much laborious tillage before they would yield fruit … they were poor men, of humble birth, low station, mean occupations … of crude condition, the twelve.[138]

Sounds like the only thing missing is a cave! I don't know about you but when I read such descriptions, I'm encouraged. Kind of sounds like me. And you, if you're honest. David gave his life to four hundred men, specifically to thirty-seven plus four. Jesus gave his time, energy, and love to twelve and most deeply to three. David and Jesus both realized their lives must have men, worshippers and warriors, who had caught their heart and vision.

Passing the Torch

It was from the twelve Jesus warriors, minus Judas, plus Paul, that the Gospel and the Kingdom of God would go forth and change the world. It is amazing what these worshippers and warriors would accomplish in the first century, under the most severe conditions. J.B. Phillips describes their passion.

> The great difference between present-day Christianity and that of which we read in these letters is that to us it is primarily a performance; to them it was a real experience. We are apt to reduce

the Christian religion to a code, or at least a rule of heart and life. To these men it is quite plainly the invasion of their lives by a new quality of life altogether. They do not hesitate to describe this as Christ living in them. Mere moral reformation will hardly explain the transformation and the exuberant vitality of these men's lives— even if we could prove a motive for such reformation, and certainly the world around offered little encouragement to the early Christians! We are practically driven to accept their own explanation, which is that their little human lives had, through Jesus Christ, been linked up with the very life of God ... These early Christians were on fire with the conviction that they had become, through Christ, literally sons of God; they were pioneers of a new humanity, founders of a new Kingdom. They still speak to us across the centuries. Perhaps if we believed what they believed, we might achieve what they achieved.[139]

Men, we are indeed pioneers of a new humanity, founders of a new Kingdom. We are being called out by Jesus to believe that our hearts matter. That our work is not more of religion but more of Jesus. More about love than law; a new work of being worshippers and warriors of a vigorous life like David *and* Jesus.

We are called by God into the heart of God, to experience the intimacy of a new identity of love. But that is not where it concludes. Most books for men end here. They get us as far as our own personal healing, our own freedom. But David's journey included the duplication of his life into other men. Jesus prepared other men for the journey ahead. That is part of the road less traveled—passing the torch to other men.

We are called by God to take this message to others. Christianity has no grandchildren. We are not born into the faith; the faith is passed down. We are grasping a torch that was passed to us and we are now in line to pass the torch to others. Paul, in his last will and testament to his son in the faith Timothy, explained the passing of the baton: "*You therefore, my son, be strong in the grace that is in Christ Jesus. And the things that you have heard from me among many witnesses, commit these to faithful men who will be able to teach others also.*"[140] Paul to Timothy, Timothy to faithful men, faithful men to others—four generations of men passing the torch!

Spiritual Fathering

For most of us, the concept of teaching others is daunting indeed. It's the overwhelming feeling I had when my first child was born. I still remember walking from the Tokyo train station to our apartment when Anna was a week old. I felt a panic attack coming on. All my joy and excitement were replaced with this thick fog of uncertainty and questioning. *Can I be a good dad? How will I do this? Where's the money going to come from?* My heart was filled with a heavy weight of dread and responsibility.

But that night something happened that changed my life. I stopped at a nearby playground, sat down, and prayed. I prayed for wisdom, power, and the presence of God. That was all I prayed for, three things—wisdom to figure this parenting thing out, power from the Holy Spirit to do it, and the presence of God to be with me. And the most amazing thing happened. (Buckle your seatbelt for what I'm going to say next … are you ready?) God answered my prayer! God showed up with wisdom, power, and presence. But not in the way I expected. It was not a Mount Sinai experience, but a gradual work of God in my heart. It was a daily journey of learning, growing, and patience. I always had just enough, and now thirty years later, all our kids are joyful, bountiful, creative men and women who love God.

But there is one key: Liz and I never parented our children alone. We needed other parents who were just a few clicks ahead of us. We asked questions, sought answers, read books, and bugged the heck out of parents we respected. We copied what we saw in parents who seemed to have joyful, free, well-adjusted kids. We were learning from them, and we found most people loved helping us.

All of us need a spiritual father, a mentor, a spiritual guide. I am now in my fifties and I have three men whom I consider spiritual guides in my life. They are all in their seventies, seasoned in life, and still loving God. Each of these men provides something I need. In his invaluable book on masculinity, Robert Hicks writes,

> Wherever I am on the masculine journey, I need a mentor who is at
> least one stage ahead of me, I need this to provide a model of
> masculinity at the next stage and the encouragement I need to leave
> where I am and grow up a little ... I need an older man who may be
> a warrior in my adult life ... I need a wounded man to come
> alongside and give me perspective I need to see that one day I may
> be the one who is bleeding ... Knowing he has survived similar
> wounding and moved on with his life may be all that I need to move
> on.[141]

We all need bloodstained allies, battle-tested brothers who love us. We
need other men in our lives who will mentor and guide us. We need robust,
joyful, vigorous men who have lived longer, lived better, lived the male
journey, who will give us the time of day. We need broken men who have
chosen not to quit, give up, or become jaded. We need that. It is the way
to growth; it is the way of the masculine journey. It is the biblical
journey—men mentoring men! It is what David gave his men; it is what
Jesus gave His disciples; it is what Paul gave Timothy.

You may not be a Paul yet, but you are most certainly a Timothy.
Timothy needed a Paul, but Timothy also needed other men he could love.
And if you are a Timothy, there are younger men in your life whom you
can spiritually father. Our churches are full of spiritually fatherless men
who have never had another man care about them. I once heard a man say
that masculinity can only be passed down by the blessing of another man.
In most of our lives, we never had that—even from our earthly fathers—
but we have it now.

That's the point of this book. Christ is our Father and Friend. He has
loved you with an eternal love; He has accepted you and calls you His
beloved. You have a good heart, a transformed heart, handed down to you
by virtue of your faith in Him. You have been given the gift of knowing
that you are beloved.

Do you realize how many men, men who call themselves Christ-
followers, have never heard the message that they are beloved? Even more
than that, do you realize how many men sit in our churches every week
who have never personally experienced their belovedness? It's largely a

message that we've never been taught.

Life on Life

What did David do that changed the lives of his men? What did Jesus do to turn his selfish, egotistical, superstitious men into fiery sons of God? What was it that Paul did to transform the timid Timothy into a man of power, love, and discipline (2 Timothy 1:6-7)? The answer is the same for each: They gave them their life.

We've been deceived in our modern Western lecture-driven schools and churches that the way of education is primarily the passing on of information. All one has to do is look at the results to see how this method falls drastically short of building real men. Instead of nurturing the heart, we have so massaged the head that we are the most educated amoral people the world has ever known. The results have been passive, insecure men who long for something more.

David, Jesus, and Paul didn't just pass on information, they passed on formation. Information fills the head, and don't get me wrong, it is important—but obedience, worship, and intimacy flow from the heart. Formation that leads to transformation is a work of life-on-life relationship through heart-to-heart love and empathy.

Just today, while sitting on my porch, I watched my ten-year old daughter playing with her seven-month old niece. They were both laughing, crawling, and carrying on with exuberance. My daughter was pouring life into her little niece. That's called life-on-life love.

That's what we can do for others. Someone has said that most things in life are more caught than taught. I agree. When we choose to love someone, care about their life, listen to their struggles, and share our heart, we are building a bond of intimacy that's transformative. They catch our heart; they catch our relationship with God.

You may not have all the Books of the Bible memorized in order; I don't. You may not know the answer to every question one might ask; I can't. You may feel extremely inadequate; I do. But you can give away what you have—your life and love relationship with Jesus. You could even start with using this book as a talking point, a diving board into one's masculinity. Why not ask God for a person you can guide, mentor, and just meet with? Use this book as a launching pad to discuss his heart, his struggles, his needs. Just give him your life and watch what God will do.

Why not live dangerously? It's your legacy.

The Dangerous Excursion: Day 21

1. Ask God for a mentor for your life. Write down three men you admire, want to emulate, and can learn from. Make a point to sit down with them and ask if they would be a bloodstained ally and mentor in your life for the next year. Whoever says yes first is your man.

2. Who is God calling you to guide, mentor, and develop? Call them, text them, and set up a time to meet together. Share with them what God is doing in your life and ask them if they would want to meet and talk through this book or do a Bible study together.

WORSHIPPER WARRIOR

For More Information on Worshipper Warrior Conferences

and

How to Follow Steve Holt:

www.steveholtonline.org

www.theroad.org

www.worshipperwarrior.org

www.facebook.com/theroadcs

https://www.facebook.com/pastorsteveholt

Twitter: @pastorsteveholt
Instagram: pastorsteveholt

ENDNOTES

1 Maxwell Maltz, *Psycho-Cybernetics: A New Way to Get More Living out of Life*, Mass Market Paperback, revised 1989, p. 134.

2 Shawn Achor, *The Happiness Advantage: Seven Principles of Positive Psychology*, Crown Business Books, New York, New York, p. 145.

3 Alan Redpath, *The Making of a Man of God*, Fleming H. Revell, Baker Book House, Grand Rapids, MI, 1962, p. 9.

4 Eugene Peterson, *Leap over a Wall* p. 6

5 The New King James Version, 1982 (1 Sa 13:14). Nashville: Thomas Nelson Publishers.

6 Deut 4: 29 NKJV

7 Eugene Peterson, *Leap Over a Wall*, Harper Collins, San Francisco, p. 206.

8 Ibid, p. 5

9 **Brené** Brown, *The Gifts of Imperfection* (Center City: Hazelden Publishing), 2010, preface.

10 Ibid

11 Brennan Manning, *The Ragamuffin Gospel* (Colorado Springs: Multonomah Publishers), 2005, p. 22-23.

12 2 Chron. 16:9 NKJV

13 1 Sam. 9:2 NKJV

14 Ps. 78:68-72 MSG

15 Ps. 34:18 NKJV

16 Alan Redpath, *The Making of a Man of God* (Ada, Michigan: Revel), 1962, p. 17-18.

17 Alan Redpath, ibid, p. 19.

18 Brennan Manning, *Abba's Child* (Colorado Springs: NavPress), 2002, p. 42.

19 Martin Lloyd Jones, *Joy Unspeakable*, (Wheaton: Harold Shaw Publishers), 1984.

20 Brennan Manning, ibid.
21 Thomas Merton, *New Seeds of Contemplation* (New York: New Directions), 1961, p. 35.
22 1 Sam. 16:13 NKJV
23 Acts 1:8 NKJV
24 Ibid, p. 22.
25 Gordon Dalbey, *Healing of the Masculine Soul* (Wheaton: Tyndale House Publishers), 1988, p. 50.
26 Ibid, p. 51.
27 1 Cor. 12:7 NKJV
28 Acts 2:3 MSG
29 Mark Batterson, *Wild Goose Chase* (Colorado Springs: Multnomah Books), 2008, Introduction.
30 George G. Hunter III, *The Celtic Way of Evangelism* (Nashville: Abingdon Press), 2000, p. 50.
31 Eph. 5:18 NKJV
32 Tim Hughes, *Here I Am to Worship* (Ventura: Revel), 2004, p. 17.
33 C.S. Lewis, *Reflections on the Psalms* (New York: Harcourt), 1958, p. 92.
34 Jack Taylor, *The Hallelujah Factor* (East Sussex: Highland Books), 1983, p. 29.:
35 C.S. Lewis, ibid, p. 96.
36 John Eldredge, *Waking the Dead* (Nashville: Thomas Nelson Publishers), 2003, p. 39.
37 John Eldredge, ibid, p. 48
38 John Eldredge, ibid, p. 69-70.
39 William Manchester, *The Last Lion, Vol. 2* (New York: Little, Brown and Company), 1984, p. 85.
40 Ibid.
41 Ibid, p. 87.
42 Ibid.
43 British Broadcasting Corporation, July 14, 1940.

44 Churchill Speech 10/29/1941; Recording on
https://www.youtube.com/watch?v=L90BCEVH41U

45 1 Sam. 17:29 NKJV

46 Logos Bible Software. Hebrew. Dabar.:

47 This concept of imagination originates with Eugene Peterson in his book *Leap Over a Wall: Earthy Spirituality for Everyday Christians* (San Francisco: HarperOne), 1998.

48 Eugene Peterson, *Leap Over a Wall: Earthy Spirituality for Everyday Christians* (San Francisco: HarperOne). 1998, p. 39

49 John Eldredge, *Wild at Heart* (Nashville: Thomas Nelson Publishers), 2001, 2010, p. 7.

50 Malcom Gladwell, *David and Goliath* (New York: Little, Brown and Company), 2013, p. 3-4.

51 1 Sam. 17:32 NKJV

52 1 Sam. 17:28 NKJV

53 Prov. 4:23 GWT

54 Gal. 5:1 NKJV

55 1 Sam. 17:32 NKJV

56 Inazo Nitobe, *Bushido: The Soul of Japan* (Tokyo: IBC Publishing), 2003, p. 27.

57 John Eldredge, *Ransomed Heart Daily Reading.* www.ransomedheart.com.

58 2 Sam. 17:47 NKJV

59 Eph. 6:12 MSG

60 Eric Metaxas, *Bonhoeffer: Pastor, Martyr, Prophet, Spy* (Nashville: Thomas Nelson Publishers), 2010, p. 241.

61 Eph. 2:2 NKJV

62 Jn. 16:33 NKJV

63 Ps. 59: Title NKJV

64 Mk. 8:33

65 Ps. 59:11 NKJV

66 Ps. 59:17 NKJV

67 Jn. 15:12-13 NKJV

68 Dictionary.com

69 Eugene Peterson, *Leap Over a Wall: Earthy Spirituality for Everyday Christians* (San Francisco: HarperOne), 1998, p. 53.

70 Dietrich Bonhoeffer, *Life Together* (San Francisco: Harper), 1954, p. 7.

71 Richard Rohr, *From Wild Man to Wise Man* (Cincinnati: St Anthony Messenger Press), 1990, p. 2.

72 Ibid.

73 Mk. 1:6 NKJV

74 1 Sam. 23:14 NKJV

75 Chris Armstrong, "*Martin Luther's Anfechtungen: His Own Dark Nights of the Soul, and How They Affected His Teaching and Ministry*," Christian History Magazine, August 24, 2011, https://gratefultothedead.wordpress.com/2011/08/24/martin-luthers-anfechtungen.

76 Zeb Bradford Long, *Passage through the Wilderness* (Grand Rapids: Chosen Books), 1998, p. 23.

77 1 Sam. 23:19 NKJV

78 1 Sam. 23:23 NKJV

79 Eugene Peterson, *Leap Over a Wall: Earthy Spirituality for Everyday Christians* (San Francisco: HarperOne), 1998, p. 72.

80 Eugene Peterson, *Leap Over a Wall: Earthy Spirituality for Everyday Christians* (San Francisco: HarperOne), 1998, p. 75.

81 Is. 55:8 NLV

82 Mtt. 7:7-8 NLV

83 Richard Rohr, *The Naked Now* (New York: A Crossroad Publishing House), 2009, p. 33.

84 Ibid, p. 34

85 **Brené** Brown, *The Gifts of Imperfection* (Center City: Hazelden Publishing), 2010, p. 39.

86 Ibid, p. 36.

87 **Brené** Brown, "*The Power of Vulnerability*," https://www.ted.com/talks/brene_brown_on_vulnerability.

88 Ibid, p. 12.

89 Ibid.

90 C.S. Lewis, *The Weight of Glory and Other Addresses, 1949.*

91 Gene Edwards, *A Tale of Three Kings* (Wheaton: Tyndale House Publishers), reprint 1992, p. 15.

92 Eugene Peterson, *Leap Over a Wall: Earthy Spirituality for Everyday Christians* (San Francisco: HarperOne), 1998, p. 77.

93 Ps. 57:1 NKJV

94 Matt Redman, *The Unquenchable Worshipper* (Ventura: Regal Books), 2001, p. 13.

95 Brennan Manning, *Abba's Child* (Colorado Springs: NavPress), 2002, p. 49.

96 Eugene Peterson, *Leap Over a Wall: Earthy Spirituality for Everyday Christians* (San Francisco: HarperOne), 1998, p. 214.

97 1 Sam. 13:14 NKJV

98 Brennan Manning, *Abba's Child* (Colorado Springs: NavPress), 2002, page 21.

99 Julian of Norwich, *The Revelations of Divine Love* (New York: Penguin), 1966, page 56.

100 Henri J.M. Nouwen, *Life of the Beloved,* New York: Crossroad, 1992, page 21.

101 Brennen Manning, ibid, p. 51.

102 Henri Nouwen, ibid, p. 26.

103 Brennen Manning, ibid, p. 52.

104 Brennan Manning, *Abba's Child,* NavPress, Colorado Springs, CO. 2002 p. 115.

105 John Eldredge, *The Journey of Desire*, Thomas Nelson Publishers, Nashville, TN, 2000, p. 8.

106 Jack Hayford, Executive Editor, *The Spirit Filled Life Bible,* Thomas Nelson, 2002, commentary on 2 Samuel 6:13-16.

107 Brené Brown, *The Gifts of Imperfection,* Hazeldon Publishing, Center City, MN. 2010, p. 78.

108 Brennan Manning, ibid, p. 97.

109 http://www.chesterton.org/who-is-this-guy/

110 Brennan Manning, ibid, p. 98.

111 William Barry, *God's Passionate Desire and our Response*, Notre Dame, IN; Ave Maria Press, 1993, p. 109.
112 Dr. Bill George, *Why Leaders Lose their Way*, Harvard Business School, internet article June, 6, 2011.
113 Ibid.
114 John Eldredge, *Wild at Heart*, Thomas Nelson Publishers, Nashville, 2000, p. 12.
115 Ibid.
116 Eugene Peterson, *Leap over a Wall*, Harper, San Francisco, 1997, p. 187
117 Ibid, p. 186.
118 Alan Redpath, The Making of a Man of God, Revel, Grand Rapids, MI, 1990, p. 242.
119 Eugene Peterson, ibib, p. 185.
120 2 Samuel 15:18 - NKJV
121 Stephen E. Ambrose, *Band of Brothers: E Company, 506th Regiment, 101st Airborne from Normandy to Hitler's Eagle's Nest*
122 Bridges, Jerry, https://www.whatchristianswanttoknow.com/christian-fellowshi-quotes-22-edifying-quotes/
123 C.J. Mahaney, *Humility, True Greatness*, Multnomah Books, Sovereign Grace Ministries, 2005, p. 22.
124 Eugene Peterson, *A Long Obedience in the Same Direction*, IVP Books, Downers Grove, IL, 2000, p. 146.
125 Timothy Keller, *Walking with God through Pain and Suffering*, Riverhead Books, New York, New York, 2013, p. 171
126 Stephen Smith, *The Jesus Life: Eight Ways to Recover Authentic Christianity*, Cook Publications, Colorado Springs, CO, 2012, p. 204.
127 Ibid, p. 204.
128 1 Peter 2:21 NIV
129 Amy Carmichael, *Poems of Amy Carmichael*, http://www.crossroad.to/Victory/poems/amy_carmichael/no-scar.htm
130 Frost, Robert, *A Boy's Will*, New York: Henry Holt and Company, 1915.

131 Walter Brueggmann, *Finally Comes the Poet*, Augsburg Fortress, Minneapolis, MN. 1989, p. 3.

132 Walt Whitman, *Leaves of Grass*

133 Henry David Thoreau, *Walden*

134 Revelation of John 11:15

135 John 7:37 *The Message*

136 Russell Whitesel, *Wholehearted, inspired by God.*

137 2 Samuel 23:8 NIV

138 A.B. Bruce, *The Training of the Twelve*, Shepherd Illustrated Classics, Keats Publishing Inc., New Canaan, Connecticut, 1979, p. 14.

139 .B. Phillips, *Letters to Young Churches,* preface.

140 2 Timothy 2:1-2 NKJV

141 Robert Hicks, *The Masculine Journey: Understanding the Six Stages of Manhood*, NavPress Publishing Group, Colorado Springs, CO, 1993, p. 179-180